全新英语阅读理解

·第一级·

主编 杨 阳

编委（按姓氏拼音排序）

程 雯 戴寅竹 胡 悦 李 晴

刘可艺 米 佳 余滨洋

中国宇航出版社

·北京·

图书在版编目（ＣＩＰ）数据

全新英语阅读理解. 第一级 / 杨阳主编. -- 北京：
中国宇航出版社，2021.12
　　ISBN 978-7-5159-1983-6

Ⅰ. ①全… Ⅱ. ①杨… Ⅲ. ①英语－语言读物 Ⅳ.
①H319.4

中国版本图书馆CIP数据核字(2021)第206948号

策划编辑　刘　杰　　　　　　封面设计　宋　航
责任编辑　刘　杰　　　　　　责任校对　冯佳佳

出　版
发　行　　中国宇航出版社

社　址　北京市阜成路8号　　　邮　编　100830
　　　　　（010）60286808　　　（010）68768548
网　址　www.caphbook.com
经　销　新华书店
发行部　（010）60286888　　　（010）68371900
　　　　　（010）60286887　　　（010）60286804（传真）
零售店　读者服务部
　　　　　（010）68371105
承　印　三河市君旺印务有限公司
版　次　2021年12月第1版　　2021年12月第1次印刷
规　格　710×1000　　　　开　本　1/16
印　张　13.5　　　　　　　字　数　250千字
书　号　ISBN 978-7-5159-1983-6
定　价　32.80元

Preface 前言

任何一门语言都需要大量的阅读，英语也不例外。阅读是吸收英语语言材料，增加语言知识，扩充词汇量的重要手段。养成良好的阅读习惯，掌握有效的阅读技巧，对小学生读者来说是非常必要的。为此，我们专门组织了一批来自一线的优秀英语教师，倾力打造了"全新英语阅读理解"系列丛书。

本系列丛书的内容是什么？

本系列丛书共四个级别，旨在通过新鲜地道的阅读素材，分年级、分层次地帮助小学生读者提升英语阅读理解能力。每个级别包含 80 篇阅读理解短文和 20 篇各地考试真题，小学生读者可以自行安排平时的练习和阶段自测。《全新英语阅读理解.第一级》适合小学三年级学生；《全新英语阅读理解.第二级》适合小学四年级学生；《全新英语阅读理解.第三级》适合小学五年级学生；《全新英语阅读理解.第四级》适合小学六年级学生。

本系列丛书的特色是什么？

内容经典

本系列丛书取材于国内外小学生经典读物，包括家庭生活、学校生活、幽默或哲理故事等单元，集可读性和趣味性于一体，激发小学生读者的阅读兴趣。

语言地道

本系列丛书摒弃带有明显中文思维痕迹的文章，特别注重语言的原汁原味，力求保证英文原文的地道性。

题型全面

本系列丛书精准解读小学阶段英语阅读理解的命题方向和规律，涵盖选择、判断和问答等常见题型，使小学生读者通过练习学会举一反三和触类旁通。

提升能力

本系列丛书栏目多样，"词汇积累"和"知识要点"侧重语言的运用；"参考译文"有助于理解原文和训练书面表达能力；"答案与解析"侧重提升思维能力和解题技巧。

英语阅读理解能力是发展其他语言技能的基础和前提。希望广大小学生读者能够用好本系列丛书，在阅读中背诵，在阅读中积累，丰富自己的知识储备，不断提升自己的英语实力。

编者

2021 年 11 月

Contents 目 录

Part 2 ★ 真题实战

Part 1
*
主题阅读

Unit 01 我和家人

 **Passage 1** 阅读短文，选择最佳答案。

Hello, I'm Tom. I'm 9 years old. Look at me! I have two big eyes and a small nose. I like blue. I can draw a dog and colour the dog blue. I can draw a pig and colour the pig pink. And I like bread and milk. This is me!

词汇积累	big /bɪg/ *adj.* 大的	small /smɔːl/ *adj.* 小的
	draw /drɔː/ *v.* 画画	pink /pɪŋk/ *adj.* 粉色的
	bread /bred/ *n.* 面包	milk /mɪlk/ *n.* 牛奶

( ) **1** How old is Tom?

    A. He is six years old.   B. He is seven years old.

    C. He is eight years old.   D. He is nine years old.

( ) **2** What does Tom look like?

    A. He has two big eyes and a big nose.

    B. He has two big eyes and a small nose.

    C. He has two small eyes and a big nose.

    D. He has two blue eyes and a small nose.

( ) **3** What colour does Tom like?

    A. Blue.   B. Red.

    C. Yellow.   D. Pink.

（　　）④ What can Tom do?

　　　　A. He can jump. 　　　　　　　B. He can fly.

　　　　C. He can sing. 　　　　　　　D. He can draw.

（　　）⑤ What does Tom like to eat?

　　　　A. Vegetables and milk. 　　　B. Bread and juice.

　　　　C. Hotdog and tea. 　　　　　D. Bread and milk.

 知识要点

　　colour作动词表示"给……上色"，例如：The children love to draw and colour.（儿童喜欢画画和涂颜色。）colour作名词表示"颜色"，例如：What colour is your coat?（你的大衣是什么颜色？）同学们还需要掌握以下单词：black（黑色），white（白色），red（红色），yellow（黄色），green（绿色）。

 参考译文

　　你好，我是汤姆。我九岁了。看我！我有两只大大的眼睛和一个小鼻子。我喜欢蓝色。我会画一只小狗并给小狗涂上蓝色。我会画一只小猪并给小猪涂上粉色。我喜欢面包和牛奶。这就是我！

 答案与解析

① D　由"I'm 9 years old."可知选D。本题考查英文单词与数字的对应。

② B　由"I have two big eyes and a small nose."可知选B。

③ A　由"I like blue."可知选A。

④ D　由"I can draw a dog and colour the dog blue. I can draw a pig and colour the pig pink."可知，汤姆会画画，D正确。

⑤ D　由"And I like bread and milk."可知选D。

 **Passage 2** 阅读短文，选择最佳答案。

My name is Mary. My mother is 35 years old. She has short hair. She is tall and beautiful. She is wearing a yellow dress and a pair of yellow shoes.

My aunt is 32 years old. She is short and pretty. She has big blue eyes. She is wearing a beautiful green dress.

词汇积累	short /ʃɔːt/ *adj.* 短的；矮的	tall /tɔːl/ *adj.* 高大的
	beautiful /ˈbjuːtɪfl/ *adj.* 美丽的	wear /weə(r)/ *v.* 穿；戴
	dress /dres/ *n.* 连衣裙	pretty /ˈprɪti/ *adj.* 美丽的

( ) ❶ How old is Mary's mother?

A. She is 35 years old.   B. She is 32 years old.

C. She is 33 years old.   D. She is 34 years old.

( ) ❷ What does Mary's mother look like?

A. She has long hair.

B. She is short and pretty.

C. She is tall and beautiful.

D. She has curly（卷的）hair.

( ) ❸ How old is Mary's aunt?

A. She is 31 years old.   B. She is 32 years old.

C. She is 33 years old.   D. She is 34 years old.

( ) ❹ What does Mary's aunt look like?

A. She has long hair.   B. She is short and pretty.

C. She is tall and beautiful.   D. She has small blue eyes.

(   ) ⑤ What does Mary's aunt wear?

A. She wears a yellow dress.

B. She wears a pair of yellow shoes.

C. She wears a beautiful green dress.

D. She wears a beautiful red dress.

 知识要点

wear表示"穿着；戴着"，强调状态，例如：She wears glasses.（她戴着眼镜。）put on表示"穿上；戴上"，强调动作，例如：She puts on her coat.（她穿上外套。）

 参考译文

我叫玛丽。我妈妈35岁。她有一头短发。她很高，很漂亮。她穿着一条黄色的连衣裙和一双黄色的鞋子。

我的小姨今年32岁。她个子不高，很漂亮。她有大大的蓝眼睛。她穿着一条漂亮的绿裙子。

 答案与解析

① A 由第一段第二句"My mother is 35 years old."可知选A。

② C 由第一段第四句"She is tall and beautiful."可知选C。

③ B 由第二段第一句"My aunt is 32 years old."可知选B。

④ B 由第二段第二句"She is short and pretty."可知选B。

⑤ C 由第二段最后一句"She is wearing a beautiful green dress."可知选C。

Passage ❸ 阅读短文，判断句子正（T）误（F）。

Hello, my name is William. This is my bedroom. You can see a desk in it. There are some books on the desk. The light is over the desk. There is also an armchair behind the desk. I can relax on it after reading or studying. The walls are white and the windows are green. You can see two pictures on one of the walls, a picture of my family and a picture of my school. My bed is near the wall. You can see some flowers under the window. My bedroom is small, but it is nice.

词汇积累		
light /laɪt/ n. 灯	armchair /'ɑːmtʃeə(r)/ n. 扶手椅
relax /rɪ'læks/ v. 放松，休息	window /'wɪndəʊ/ n. 窗户

( ) ❶ There are two desks in William's bedroom.

( ) ❷ The books are on the desk.

( ) ❸ William likes to relax on the armchair.

( ) ❹ There is a picture of William's friends on the wall.

( ) ❺ There are nine kinds of things in William's bedroom.

 知识要点

one of 表示"其中之一"，动词用单数形式。例如：He is one of my best friends.（他是我最好的朋友之一。）It's one of my favourite movies.（这是我最喜欢的电影之一。）

 参考译文

　　你好，我叫威廉。这是我的卧室。你可以看到里面有一张书桌。桌子上有一些书。灯在桌子的正上方。桌子后面还有一把扶手椅。阅读或学习后，我可以在上面放松一下。墙壁是白色的，窗户是绿色的。你可以在一面墙上看到两张照片，一张是我家人的照片，另一张是我学校的照片。我的床靠近墙。你可以看到窗户下面有一些花。我的卧室很小，却很温馨。

 答案与解析

　　1 F　由 "You can see a desk in it." 可知，威廉的房间里有一张桌子，不是两张，本题错误。

　　2 T　由 "There are some books on the desk." 可知本题正确。

　　3 T　由 "I can relax on it after reading or studying." 可知，"it" 指代前文中的 "armchair"，本题正确。

　　4 F　由 "You can see two pictures on one of the walls, a picture of my family and a picture of my school." 可知本题错误。

　　5 T　威廉提到了自己卧室里的桌子、书、灯、扶手椅、墙、窗户、照片、床和鲜花，一共九种物品，本题正确。

 Passage **4**　阅读短文，判断句子正（T）误（F）。

　　Bill is an English boy. He is twelve. He lives with his family in China. There are four people in his family. They are his father Jack Clinton, his mother Catherine, and his little sister Abby. He has

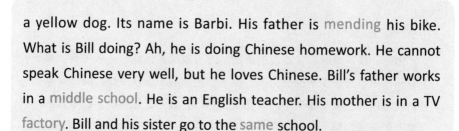

a yellow dog. Its name is Barbi. His father is mending his bike. What is Bill doing? Ah, he is doing Chinese homework. He cannot speak Chinese very well, but he loves Chinese. Bill's father works in a middle school. He is an English teacher. His mother is in a TV factory. Bill and his sister go to the same school.

词汇 积累	mend /mend/ v. 修理，修补	middle school 中学
	factory /ˈfæktri/ n. 工厂	same /seɪm/ adj. 相同的

(　　) ❶ Bill is a twelve-year-old English boy.

(　　) ❷ Bill lives in China with his grandparents.

(　　) ❸ There are five people in Bill's family.

(　　) ❹ Bill is doing his Chinese homework.

(　　) ❺ Bill's mother is an English teacher.

 知识要点

　　English作名词表示"英语"，例如：She speaks good English.（她英语说得很好。）English作形容词表示"英语的；英国的；英国人的"，例如：This is an English dictionary.（这是一本英语词典。）The English countryside is very beautiful.（英国的乡村很美丽。）

 参考译文

　　比尔是个英国男孩，他12岁。他与家人住在中国。他家有四口人，他的爸爸杰克·克林顿，他的妈妈凯瑟琳和他的妹妹阿比。他有一只黄色的

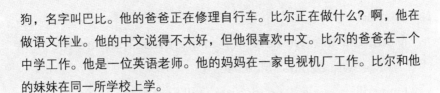
狗，名字叫巴比。他的爸爸正在修理自行车。比尔正在做什么？啊，他在做语文作业。他的中文说得不太好，但他很喜欢中文。比尔的爸爸在一个中学工作。他是一位英语老师。他的妈妈在一家电视机厂工作。比尔和他的妹妹在同一所学校上学。

 答案与解析

❶ T　由第一句和第二句可知本题正确。

❷ F　由全文可知，比尔和家人住在中国，比尔家里有四口人，爸爸、妈妈和妹妹，并没有提到祖父母，本题错误。

❸ F　由 "There are four people in his family." 可知本题错误。

❹ T　由 "What is Bill doing? Ah, he is doing Chinese homework." 可知本题正确。

❺ F　由 "Bill's father works in a middle school. He is an English teacher. His mother is in a TV factory." 可知本题错误。

 Passage 5 阅读短文，判断句子正（T）误（F）。

My Three Sisters

My name is Tasha. I have three sisters. We look a lot alike. We all have brown eyes and brown hair.

I am the youngest. But I am very tall. I am taller than one of my older sisters. I ask my mom why. She says that it's because Dad is tall. His parents are both tall too. Mom is shorter. She says I am tall like Dad.

Mom says that we have her colour eyes. They are the same shade of brown. Dad has blue eyes.

I am still growing. I wonder how tall I am going to be.

词汇 积累	alike /əˈlaɪk/ *adj.* 相像的，相似的	both /bəʊθ/ *pron.* 两个，两个都
	shade /ʃeɪd/ *n.* 色度	wonder /ˈwʌndə(r)/ *v.* 想知道

( ) ❶ Tasha looks different from her sisters.

( ) ❷ Tasha is the youngest.

( ) ❸ Tasha is taller than her three sisters.

( ) ❹ Tasha and her mom have brown eyes.

( ) ❺ Tasha's father has brown eyes.

 知识要点

　　shade的常用意思是"树荫，阴凉处"，例如：Let's sit in the shade for a while.（咱们在阴凉处坐一会儿吧。）shade在文中表示"色度，浓淡深浅"，例如：We like the same shade of green.（我们喜欢这个色度的绿色。）

 参考译文

我的三个姐姐

　　我叫塔莎。我有三个姐姐。我们长得很像。我们都有棕色的眼睛和棕色的头发。

我是最小的。但是我很高。我比我的一个姐姐还高。我问妈妈为什么。她说那是因为爸爸个子高。他的父母也都很高。妈妈要矮一些。她说我个子高随爸爸。

妈妈说我们的眼睛和她的眼睛颜色一样。它们是同样深浅的棕色。爸爸的眼睛是蓝色的。

我还在长个子。我想知道我能长多高。

 答案与解析

❶ F 由第一段可知，塔莎有三个姐姐，她们长得很像，本题错误。

❷ T 由第二段第一句可知本题正确。

❸ F 由第二段第三句可知，塔莎比她的一个姐姐个子高，而不是题中所说的比三个姐姐都要高，本题错误。

❹ T 由第三段前两句可知本题正确。

❺ F 由第三段最后一句可知，塔莎的爸爸的眼睛是蓝色的，本题错误。

 Passage 6 阅读短文，选择最佳答案。

It's time for Tom to go to school. Classes begin at 7:40. Tom is still in his room. His mother says, "Hurry, Tom. You must be quick or you will be late." "Mum, where's my pencil box? I can't find it. I can't go to school without my pencil box." cries Tom. Look at Tom's room. What a mess! His books are lying all over the room. His football socks are on the desk. A kite and some clothes are on his bed. Tom's mother comes to help him. She asks Tom to put his

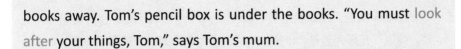

books away. Tom's pencil box is under the books. "You must look after your things, Tom," says Tom's mum.

词汇 积累	begin /bɪ'gɪn/ *v.* 开始	hurry /'hʌri/ *v.* 赶快，急忙（做某事）
	quick /kwɪk/ *adj.* 迅速的	mess /mes/ *n.* 肮脏，杂乱
	lie /laɪ/ *v.* 位于，平放	look after 照顾，照管

( ) ❶ When do classes begin?

    A. Classes begin at 7: 40.   B. Classes begin at 8: 40.

    C. Classes begin at 7: 30.   D. Classes begin at 7: 50.

( ) ❷ Why is Tom still in his room?

    A. Because he does not want to go to school.

    B. Because he cannot find his pencil box.

    C. Because he cannot find his books.

    D. Because he cries.

( ) ❸ How does Tom feel?

    A. He feels happy.   B. He feels great.

    C. He feels good.   D. He feels sad.

( ) ❹ What do you know about Tom's room?

    A. His room is clean.   B. His room is messy.

    C. His room is beautiful.   D. His room is good.

( ) ❺ What should Tom do?

    A. He should put the kite on the bed.

    B. He should put the socks on the floor.

    C. He should look after his things.

    D. He should ask his mother to help him.

 知识要点

It's time to do sth. 表示"该做……了。"例如：It's time to do your homework.（你该做作业了。）It's time to play basketball.（该打篮球了。）

 参考译文

汤姆该上学了。七点四十开始上课。汤姆还在他的房间里。他的妈妈说："赶快，汤姆。你快点，不然就迟到了。""妈妈，我的铅笔盒在哪呢？我找不到它。我不能不带铅笔盒就去学校。"汤姆喊道。看看汤姆的房间。真是一团糟！他的书摆得满地都是。他的足球袜在书桌上。床上放着一个风筝和一些衣服。汤姆的妈妈过来帮他。她让汤姆把他的书放到一边去。汤姆的铅笔盒就在书底下。"你必须照看好你自己的东西，汤姆。"汤姆的妈妈说道。

 答案与解析

❶ A   由第二句"Classes begin at 7:40."可知选A。

❷ B   由汤姆和妈妈对话时说的"I can't go to school without my pencil box."可知选B。

❸ D   根据文章大意，到了该上学的时间，汤姆因为找不到铅笔盒而大喊大叫，因此汤姆的心情是不开心的，D正确。

❹ B   由"Look at Tom's room. What a mess!"可知，汤姆的房间很乱，"messy"是"mess"的形容词形式，表示"脏乱的"，B正确。

❺ C   由最后一句"'You must look after your things, Tom,' says Tom's mum."可知选C。

Unit 02　学校生活

 Passage 1 阅读短文，回答问题。

My school is big and beautiful. There are forty-two classrooms in our school. Our classroom is on the fourth floor. There are two table tennis rooms on the first floor. There are four music rooms on the third floor. We have music lessons there. There are three art rooms on the third floor too. There are two playgrounds in our school. They are big. We can play football there. I love my school very much.

词汇积累	table tennis 乒乓球	music /'mjuːzɪk/ n. 音乐
	art /ɑːt/ n. 美术，艺术	playground /'pleɪɡraʊnd/ n. 操场

1 How many classrooms are there in the school?

_____

2 What kind of room can you find on the first floor?

_____

3 Where are the music rooms?

_____

4 How many playgrounds are there in the school?

_____

5 What can we do on the playground?

_____

 **知识要点**

There be句型表示"某地有某人或某物"，谓语动词be有时态和单复数的变化。例如：There is an apple in the bag.（包里有一个苹果。）There was a puppet show yesterday.（昨天有一场木偶表演。）

 参考译文

我的学校又大又漂亮。我们学校有42个教室。我们的教室在四楼。一楼有两个乒乓球室。三楼有四个音乐室。我们在那里上音乐课。三楼也有三个美术室。我们学校有两个操场。它们很大。我们可以在那里踢足球。我非常爱我的学校。

 答案与解析

① Forty-two. 由第二句"There are forty-two classrooms in our school."可知答案。

② Table tennis room. 由第四句"There are two table tennis rooms on the first floor."可知答案。

③ They are on the third floor. 由第五句"There are four music rooms on the third floor."可知答案。

④ Two. 由倒数第四句"There are two playgrounds in our school."可知答案。

⑤ We can play football there. 由倒数第二句可知答案。

Passage   阅读短文，判断句子正（T）误（F）。

I am in China now. I go to school five days a week. The school and the food are good here. I have some Chinese friends. They are all very friendly to me. On Saturdays and Sundays we stay at home. In the afternoon we play games. My Chinese friends like English very much. They ask me to teach them English and they teach me Chinese. I like staying here.

词汇积累	friendly /'fren(d)li/ *adj.* 友好的	Saturday /'sætədeɪ/ *n.* 星期六
	Sunday /'sʌndeɪ/ *n.* 星期日	stay /steɪ/ *v.* 待，停留
	ask /ɑːsk/ *v.* 要求，请求	teach /tiːtʃ/ *v.* 教

(　　) ① I come from China.

(　　) ② I go to school everyday.

(　　) ③ I like the food in China.

(　　) ④ I don't have friends at school.

(　　) ⑤ I teach my friends English.

 知识要点

ask sb. to do sth. 表示"请求某人做某事"，例如：Mom asked me to help her with the dishes. （妈妈让我帮她洗碗。）The kid asked me to play with him. （那个小孩让我和他玩。）

Unit 02 学校生活

参考译文

我现在在中国。我每周有五天去学校上学。这里的学校和食物都很不错。我有一些中国朋友。他们对我都非常友好。在周六和周日，我们会待在家里。下午我们会一起玩游戏，我的中国朋友很喜欢英语。他们让我教他们英语，他们教我中文。我喜欢待在这里。

 **答案与解析**

① F　由第一句"I am in China now."可知，本题与原文不符。

② F　由第二句"I go to school five days a week."可知，"我"每周有五天去上学，不是每天都去上学，本题错误。

③ T　由第三句"The school and the food are good here."可知，"我"喜欢这里的食物，本题正确。

④ F　由第四句和第五句"I have some Chinese friends. They are all very friendly to me."可知，本题与原文不符。

⑤ T　由倒数第二句"They ask me to teach them English and they teach me Chinese."可知本题正确。

 Passage 3 阅读短文，判断句子正（T）误（F）。

My School

Hi! My name is Hanna. I live in a small town. My school is on 11 Apple Road. The road has a lot of houses and trees.

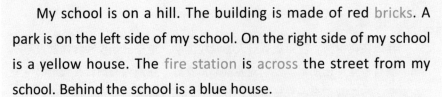

My school is on a hill. The building is made of red bricks. A park is on the left side of my school. On the right side of my school is a yellow house. The fire station is across the street from my school. Behind the school is a blue house.

The blue house is on Valley Street. My house is at the end of that street. I am close enough to walk to school!

词汇 积累	town /taʊn/ *n.* 城镇	brick /brɪk/ *n.* 砖块
	fire station 消防站	across /ə'krɒs/ *prep.* 在……对面
	valley /'væli/ *n.* 山谷	close /kləʊs/ *adj.* 靠近的

(   ) ❶ Hanna lives in a big city.

(   ) ❷ Hanna's school is on a hill.

(   ) ❸ The fire station is on 11 Apple Road.

(   ) ❹ The blue house is on Valley Street.

(   ) ❺ Hanna goes to school by bus.

 知识要点

be made of表示"由……制成"（通常能看出原材料），例如：The kite is made of paper.（风筝是用纸做的。）be made from也表示"由……制成"（通常看不出原材料），例如：The paper is made from wood.（纸是木头做的。）

参考译文

我的学校

嗨！我叫汉娜。我住在一个小镇上。我的学校在苹果路11号。马路上有很多房子和树。

我的学校在小山上。学校大楼是用红砖建成的。在我学校的左边是一个公园。在我学校的右边是一座黄色的房子。消防站在我们学校的街对面。学校后面是一座蓝色的房子。

蓝房子在山谷街上。我家在那条街的尽头。我离学校很近，可以走路去上学！

答案与解析

❶ F 由第一段第三句 "I live in a small town." 可知本题错误。

❷ T 由第二段第一句 "My school is on a hill." 可知本题正确。

❸ T 由第一段第四句 "My school is on 11 Apple Road." 以及第二段倒数第二句 "The fire station is across the street from my school." 可知，消防站在学校对面，推测出也在同一条路上，本题正确。

❹ T 由第三段第一句 "The blue house is on Valley Street." 可知本题正确。

❺ F 由第三段最后一句 "I am close enough to walk to school!" 可知本题错误。

 Passage 4 阅读短文，选择最佳答案。

You work hard to learn English. Do you know American kids are learning Chinese? In many US schools, students take Chinese lessons. How do they learn Chinese? Let us go to the Muir Elementary School（小学）in the US. Maddy, 6, and Stephen, 6, are first graders in this school. They are learning how to say "we" in Chinese. "It's not easy to remember Chinese characters. But learning Chinese is fun," they say.

In Chinese class, they are learning the language through songs, games, and lots of talking. "Chinese is popular among US kids. They pick it up really fast," their teacher says.

词汇积累		
	elementary /ˌelɪˈmentri/	grader /ˈɡreɪdə(r)/
	adj. 基本的，初级的	n. 特定年级的学生
	remember /rɪˈmembə(r)/	character /ˈkærəktə(r)/
	v. 记住	n. 文字
	through /θruː/	popular /ˈpɒpjələ(r)/
	prep. 凭借，通过	adj. 受欢迎的

( ) ❶ What do you know about American kids?

A. They do not learn English.

B. They do not learn Chinese.

C. They learn Chinese.

D. They do not like Chinese.

(   ) ❷ How many students are mentioned in this text?

    A. Two.   B. Three.

    C. One.   D. Four.

(   ) ❸ How do American students think about Chinese?

    A. They think Chinese is easy.

    B. They think Chinese is fun.

    C. They think Chinese is boring.

    D. They think Chinese character is not hard to remember.

(   ) ❹ How do American students learn Chinese?

    A. They learn Chinese through songs.

    B. They learn Chinese through games.

    C. They learn Chinese through lots of talking.

    D. All the above are right.

(   ) ❺ What do you know from this text?

    A. American students learn Chinese really fast.

    B. American students learn Chinese because it is popular.

    C. American students learn Chinese through reading.

    D. American students take Chinese lessons after school.

知识要点

pick up表示"不费力地学会"，例如：Where did you pick up your English?（你是在哪儿学的英语？）She picked up Chinese when she was living in China.（她旅居中国时顺便学会了中文。）

参考译文

你学习英语很努力。你知道美国孩子也在学习中文吗？在许多美国学校里，学生会上中文课。他们如何学习中文呢？让我们走进美国的缪尔小学。六岁的马迪和斯蒂芬是这所学校的一年级学生。他们正在学习怎么用中文说"我们"。"中国字不好记。但是学中文很有意思。"他们说。

在中文课上，他们通过唱歌、做游戏和进行大量的对话来学习这门语言。"中文在美国孩子中很流行。他们学得很快。"他们的老师说。

 答案与解析

❶ C　由第一段第二句和第三句可知选C。文中并未提及A，B与原文不符，由第一段最后一句可知美国孩子认为学中文有意思，排除D。

❷ A　由第一段第六句可知，提到了马迪和斯蒂芬两位同学，A正确。

❸ B　由第一段最后一句可知选B。A、C、D均与原文不符。

❹ D　由第二段第一句可知选D。A、B、C均不全面。

❺ A　由第二段第二句可知选A。根据原文，中文流行并不是美国学生学中文的原因，排除B。C和D在文中并未提及。

 Passage **5** 阅读短文，判断句子正（T）误（F）。

It's September and we are back to school. It's good to see all my classmates and teachers again. They are all fine and happy. We are in Grade Eight this term. There are twenty-six girls and twenty-eight boys in our class.

Mr. Hu is our new English teacher and Mr. Li will teach us physics. Physics is a new subject. I hear physics is not easy, but it's interesting. I'm going to work hard on it. I'm good at math, but I don't do well in English. I like English. I'll ask Lucy for help.

Lucy is my good friend and I can help her with her Chinese, too. I'm going to do my best this term. I think I can do better than last term.

词汇积累	term /tɜrm/ *n.* 学期	physics /'fɪzɪks/ *n.* 物理
	subject /'sʌbdʒɪkt/ *n.* 学科	hear /hɪə(r)/ *v.* 听说

(   ) **1** We were in Grade Seven last term.

(   ) **2** Mr. Hu is our new math teacher.

(   ) **3** We don't have physics this term.

(   ) **4** I'm good at math and English.

(   ) **5** Lucy is good at English.

 知识要点

be good at表示"擅长……，"后面跟名词、代词或动词的ing形式。例如：He is good at English.（他擅长英语。）I'm good at drawing.（我擅长画画。）

 参考译文

现在是九月，我们回到学校了。再次见到我所有的同学和老师真是太好了。他们都很好，很快乐。这学期我们上八年级。我们班有26个女孩和28个男孩。

胡老师是我们的新英语老师，李老师将教我们物理。物理是一门新学科。我听说物理不容易，但它很有趣。我要努力学习。我数学学得好，但英语学得不好。我喜欢英语。我会找露西帮忙的。

露西是我的好朋友，我也可以帮助她学习中文。这学期我要尽最大努力学习。我想我能比上学期做得更好。

 答案与解析

❶ T 由第一段第四句可推测，上学期是七年级，本题正确。

❷ F 由第二段第一句可知，胡老师是我们的新英语老师，而不是数学老师，本题错误。

❸ F 由第二段第二句可知本题错误。

❹ F 由第二段倒数第三句可知本题错误。

❺ T 由第二段最后一句可知，"我"英语不好的时候会找露西寻求帮助，因此可推测露西的英语很好，本题正确。

 Passage   阅读短文，选择最佳答案。

Jim wants to borrow a book from a new library. He comes to the library with Wang Jin. They cannot see any assistants, but some robots standing there. Then Jim says to the robot, "Hey, give me the book." But the robot does not move.

"What's wrong with the robot?" he asks Wang Jin.

Wang Jin tells him, "When you want to borrow something from somebody, you must say 'please' first."

So Jim says, "Please give the book to me, Mr. Robot." Then the

robot brings him the book. But again, Jim cannot take the book out of the robot's hands.

Wang Jin says, "You must say 'Thank you' before you take the book." So Jim says, "Oh, thank you very much." Then the robot gives the book to him.

词汇 积累	borrow /'bɒrəʊ/ v. 借，借用	library /'laɪbrəri/ n. 图书馆
	assistant /ə'sɪstənt/ n. 助理	robot /'rəʊbɒt/ n. 机器人
	move /muːv/ v. 移动	bring /brɪŋ/ v. 带来，取来

(　　) ❶ What does Jim want to do?

      A. Jim wants to go out with Wang Jin.

      B. Jim wants to buy a robot.

      C. Jim wants to buy a book.

      D. Jim wants to borrow a book.

(　　) ❷ Why cannot they see any assistants in the library?

      A. Because the library does not open today.

      B. Because the assistants of this library are the robots.

      C. Because the assistants in the library are having lunch.

      D. Because all the assistants are gone.

(　　) ❸ In the first paragraph（段）, why does the robot not move?

      A. Because it does not work.

      B. Because it does not understand what Jim says.

      C. Because Jim does not say "please" first.

      D. Because Jim breaks it.

( ) ④ Why cannot Jim take the book out of the robot's hands?

    A. Because Jim does not say "Thank you" before he takes the book.

    B. Because Jim does not give money to the robot.

    C. Because Jim does not say "Please" before he takes the book.

    D. Because there is something wrong with the robot.

( ) ⑤ What do you know from this text?

    A. The new library is not good.

    B. We should say politely to others.

    C. The robot does not work very well.

    D. Jim does not borrow a book.

 知识要点

    borrow表示"借"，所借的东西要到说话者手里来。例如：Can I borrow your umbrella?（借你的伞用一下行吗？）而lend表示"借给，借出"，所借的东西要远离说话者而去。例如：I lent the car to a friend.（我把车借给了一位朋友。）

 参考译文

    吉姆想从一个新图书馆借一本书。他和王进一起去图书馆。他们没有看到任何助理，却只看到了一些站在那里的机器人。然后吉姆对机器人说："嘿，给我这本书。"但是这个机器人没有动。

    "这个机器人怎么了？"他问王进。

    王进告诉他："当你想从某人那里借某样东西的时候，你应该先说'请'。"

    于是吉姆说："请把这本书给我，机器人先生。"然后机器人给他带来了这本书。但是这一次，吉姆不能从机器人的手中拿到这本书。

    王进说："你拿书之前必须说'谢谢'。"因此吉姆说："哦，非常感谢您。"然后机器人把书给了他。

 答案与解析

❶ D 由第一段第一句可知选D。

❷ B 结合全文可知，机器人就是图书馆助理，B正确。图书馆已经开门了，A错误。文中并未提及图书馆助理是否去吃午饭或者离开，C和D错误。

❸ C 由第三段可知，由于吉姆第一次没有说礼貌用语"请"，所以机器人没有动，C正确。

❹ A 由最后一段王进说的话可知，吉姆应该使用礼貌用语"谢谢"，A正确。吉姆是去图书馆借书，不用给钱，B错误。当你想从某人那里借某样东西的时候，你应该先说"请"。而吉姆现在是拿东西，C错误。机器人没有出故障，只是因为吉姆没有说礼貌用语，D错误。

❺ B 结合全文，吉姆使用礼貌用语后才借到了书，说明我们与人交流时要使用礼貌用语，B正确。

 **Passage 7** 阅读短文，选择最佳答案。

Greg Heffley is an 11-year-old boy. He is kind, honest, smart, and naughty. He has a lot of ideas. He keeps a diary. In his diary, he writes many interesting stories about his life. He also draws pictures in his diary. He has a lot of problems in school and makes a lot of troubles. He often wants to play tricks on others. But he always makes fool of himself. He is not good at making friends. But he wants to be the most popular in his school.

Greg is not a good role model. But US children like reading his diaries. In fact, everything Greg does, you should do the opposite.

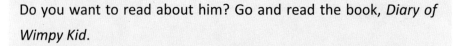

Do you want to read about him? Go and read the book, *Diary of Wimpy Kid.*

词汇 积累	honest /'ɒnɪst/ *adj.* 诚实的	smart /smɑːt/ *adj.* 聪明的
	naughty /'nɔːti/ *adj.* 顽皮的	idea /aɪ'dɪə/ *n.* 主意
	problem /'prɒbləm/ *n.* 难题	trouble /'trʌbl/ *n.* 麻烦
	role model 楷模，榜样	opposite /'ɒpəzɪt/ *n.* 对立面

( ) ❶ What kind of person is Greg Heffley?

    A. He is a bad person.   B. He is a kind person.

    C. He is popular.   D. He is a good role model.

( ) ❷ What does Greg Heffley do at school?

    A. He listens to teacher carefully.

    B. He does not have problems.

    C. He likes to play tricks on others.

    D. He is good at making friends.

( ) ❸ What does Greg Heffley want?

    A. He wants to keep a diary.

    B. He wants to be a role model.

    C. He wants to go home.

    D. He wants to be the most popular.

( ) ❹ Why do US children read Greg Heffley's diary?

    A. Because the diary is very interesting.

    B. Because they can do the same thing in the diary.

    C. Because Greg Heffley is popular.

    D. Because their parents want them to read this diary.

(   ) 5 What is the best title（标题）of this text?

A. The Diary of Greg Heffley

B. Be Away from Greg Heffley

C. The Bad Child—Greg Heffley

D. Greg Heffley's School Life

 知识要点

　　play tricks on sb.表示"捉弄某人"，例如：It's a tradition to play tricks on others on April Fool's Day.（在愚人节那天捉弄别人是一个传统。）make fool of sb.表示"愚弄某人"，例如：We all make fool of ourselves at times.（我们有时都会做傻事。）

 参考译文

　　格雷格·赫弗莱是一个11岁的男孩。他善良、诚实、聪明又顽皮。他想法很多，还写日记。在日记中，他写了许多关于自己生活的有趣故事。他还在日记里画画。他在学校遇到了很多问题，也惹了很多麻烦。他经常捉弄别人，但最后总是捉弄了自己。他不善于交朋友，但却想成为学校中最受欢迎的人。

　　格雷格不是个好榜样。但是美国孩子喜欢看他的日记。实际上，格雷格所做的一切，你们都应该反着做。你想看看他的故事吗？去读《小屁孩日记》吧。

 答案与解析

　　1 B　由第一段第二句可知，格雷格并不坏，只是有些顽皮，A错误，B正确。由第一段最后一句可知，格雷格想变得最受欢迎，所以他还不是最受欢迎的孩子，C错误。由第二段第一句可知D错误。

❷ C 由第一段倒数第四句可知选C。A在文中并未提及，B和D均与文意相反。

❸ D 由第一段最后一句可知选D。格雷格已经写日记了，A错误。文中只是指出格雷格不是个好的榜样，B错误。文中没有提及格雷格是否想回家，C错误。

❹ A 由第一段第五句可知，格雷格的日记记录了很多有趣的事情，可以推测这是美国孩子喜欢看他日记的原因。由第二段第三句可知B错误，由第一段最后一句可知C错误，D在文中并未提及。

❺ A 本文重点介绍了格雷格和他的日记，A正确。文中并未提及是否要远离格雷格，B错误。格雷格本质不坏，只是有些淘气，C错误。本文并不是在详细介绍格雷格的学校生活，D错误。

Unit 03 饮食与健康

Americans usually eat three meals a day. Breakfast usually comes before eight o'clock in the morning. They usually have eggs, some meat, bread, fruit juice and coffee. Lunch is between twelve and one o'clock. It is like a light meal and working people must take lunch with them or get it near workplace.

Children in school take sandwiches, fruit, and cookies with them or eat in school. Supper, the main meal, is between six and eight in the evening. People cook it carefully. They may have meat such as chicken, turkey, and duck. They may have potatoes or rice, vegetables or salad. The drink is coffee, tea, or milk. Then comes the dessert.

词汇积累	meal /miːl/ *n.* 早（或午、晚）餐 workplace /ˈwɜːkpleɪs/ *n.* 工作场所 salad /ˈsæləd/ *n.* 沙拉	between /bɪˈtwiːn/ *prep.* （时间上）在……之间 supper /ˈsʌpə(r)/ *n.* 晚餐 dessert /dɪˈzɜːt/ *n.* （饭后）甜点

( ) ❶ Which kind of food is the breakfast of Americans?

    A. Rice.   B. Duck.

    C. Turkey.   D. Bread.

( ) ❷ When do Americans usually have lunch?

    A. They have lunch at 12:40.

    B. They have lunch at 11:30.

    C. They have lunch at 13:10.

    D. They have lunch at 11:50.

( ) ❸ How do children usually have lunch in school days?

    A. They go home to have lunch.

    B. They eat in school.

    C. They buy food in school.

    D. They don't have lunch.

( ) ❹ Which one is right about supper?

    A. Supper is the main meal.

    B. Americans have supper at 8:30.

    C. Americans eat turkey at breakfast.

    D. Americans eat dessert before supper.

( ) ❺ What is the best title of this passage?

    A. The Main Meal

    B. Healthy Meals in America

    C. Meals of Americans

    D. American Supper

 知识要点

    light在文中作形容词，表示"（食物、膳食）少量而易消化的"，例如：I just want something light for lunch.（我午饭稍微吃点就够了。）light meal表示"量少而便于携带的一餐"，即"便餐"。

参考译文

　　美国人通常一日三餐。早餐通常在早晨八点前。他们一般吃鸡蛋、一些肉、面包，喝果汁和咖啡。午餐在十二点至一点之间。午餐为便餐，有工作的人必须自带午餐，或者在工作地点附近解决午餐。

　　上学的孩子会自带三明治、水果和饼干作为午餐，他们也可以在学校吃午餐。晚餐是正餐，在晚上六点至八点之间。人们一般会用心准备。他们会吃鸡肉、火鸡肉和鸭肉等肉类，也会吃土豆或米饭、蔬菜或沙拉。饮品包括咖啡、茶或牛奶。晚餐之后是甜点。

答案与解析

🄳 **D** 　由第一段第三句可知选D。A、B、C均是美国人晚餐时吃的食物。

🄐 **A** 　由第一段第四句可知美国人的午餐在十二点至一点之间，A正确。

🄑 **B** 　由第二段第一句可知选B。学生会自带午餐或者在学校用餐，排除D；学生不回家吃午餐，排除A；C在文中并未提及。

🄐 **A** 　由第二段第二句可知A正确而B错误。由第二段第四句可知晚餐吃火鸡，C错误，由第二段最后一句可知D错误。

🄒 **C** 　本文主要介绍了美国人一日三餐的食物、时间和食用方式，C符合文章大意。

Passage ❷ 　阅读短文，选择最佳答案。

　　Look at all the kinds of drinks on the table. There is tea, water, fruit juice, milk and fizzy drinks. What should you drink? Coke tastes great, but it is really bad for your teeth and bones. It has a lot of sugar. Some drinks are good for you. Some are not. The health experts tell you to drink water and milk. Your body needs lots of water. Milk is good for your eyes and bones.

词汇积累	fizzy drinks 起泡饮料，汽水	taste /teɪst/ v. 尝起来
	bone /bəʊn/ n. 骨头	health expert 健康专家

(　　) ❶ How many kinds of drinks on the table?

A. There are four kinds of drinks.

B. There are five kinds of drinks.

C. There are six kinds of drinks.

D. There are seven kinds of drinks.

(　　) ❷ Which one is wrong about coke?

A. It tastes bad.　　　　　　　　　B. It is bad for us.

C. It is bad for our teeth.　　　　　D. It has a lot of sugar.

(　　) ❸ What do health experts tell us to drink?

A. They tell us to drink coke.

B. They tell us to drink fruit juice.

C. They tell us to drink milk.

D. They tell us to drink fizzy drinks.

(　　) ❹ Milk is good for your _____.

A. ears　　　　　　　　　　　　　B. head

C. mouth　　　　　　　　　　　　D. bones

(　　) ❺ What should we do after reading this passage?

A. We should drink a lot of coke.

B. We shouldn't drink fruit juice.

C. We should drink water and milk.

D. Don't drink tea.

 知识要点

be bad for表示"对……不利,对……有害",例如:Too much drink is bad for your health.(饮酒过度对你的健康有害。)be good for表示"有益于……,对……有好处",例如:Vegetables are good for your health.(蔬菜对你的健康有益。)

 参考译文

看看桌子上的各种饮料,有茶、水、果汁、牛奶和汽水。你应该喝什么?可乐很好喝,但是它对你的牙和骨头非常有害。它含糖太多。一些饮料对你有益。一些饮料对你有害。健康专家建议你喝水和牛奶。你的身体需要大量的水。牛奶对你的眼睛和骨头有益。

 答案与解析

❶ B 由第二句可知,桌子上有茶、水、果汁、牛奶和汽水,一共五种饮料,B正确。

❷ A 由第四句和第五句可知,B、C、D均正确,只有A不符合原文。

❸ C 由倒数第三句可知选C。A、B、D在文中均未提及。

❹ D 由最后一句可知选D。

❺ C 结合全文,可乐对我们的健康有害,排除A;B、D在文中均未提及。健康专家建议我们喝水和牛奶,C正确。

 Passage **3** 阅读短文，判断句子正（T）误（F）。

Little Freddie was having trouble in school. His mom was worried. So she took Freddie to see a doctor.

Dr. Adams gave him an eye test. He told Freddie that he did not see as well as the other kids.

"Your eyes are weak," said Dr. Adams. "You have trouble seeing what the teacher writes on the board. That's why you need to get eyeglasses."

"Oh no!" Freddie cried. "I don't want to wear glasses. The kids will make fun of me."

"Don't you want to do better in school?" His mom said.

The doctor said, "You have a problem with your eyesight. Wearing glasses will help prevent（阻止）it from getting worse. Some people can even go blind if they don't wear glasses."

词汇积累	test /test/ *n.* 测试	weak /wiːk/ *adj.* 弱的
	write /raɪt/ *v.* 写	eyesight /'aɪsaɪt/ *n.* 视力

(　　) ❶ Freddie's mom took him to see a doctor because he was ill.

(　　) ❷ The doctor suggested（建议）that Freddie should not watch TV.

(　　) ❸ Freddie doesn't want to wear glasses because other kids will make fun of him.

(　　) ❹ According to the doctor, wearing glasses is very cool.

(　　) ❺ If Freddie doesn't wear glasses, he might go blind in the future.

知识要点

make fun of sb.表示"取笑某人",例如:They make fun of the new student.(他们取笑新同学。)Don't make fun of him.(别拿他开玩笑。)

 参考译文

小弗雷迪在学校遇到了麻烦。他的妈妈很担心,于是带弗雷迪去看了医生。

亚当斯医生给他做了视力检查。他告诉弗雷迪,他不像其他孩子看得那么清楚。

"你的眼睛不好,"亚当斯医生说。"你看不清老师在黑板上写的东西。这就是为什么你需要戴眼镜。"

"噢,不!"弗雷迪哭了。"我不想戴眼镜。孩子们会取笑我的。"

"你难道不想在学校表现得更好吗?"他的妈妈说。

医生说:"你的视力有问题。戴眼镜有助于防止视力变得更差。有些人如果不戴眼镜甚至会失明。"

 答案与解析

❶ F 由第二段第二句可知,因为弗雷迪视力不好,所以妈妈带他去看医生,本题错误。

❷ F 由第三段最后一句可知,医生建议弗雷迪配戴眼镜,本题错误。

❸ T 由第四段弗雷迪说的话可知,他不想戴眼镜是害怕其他孩子嘲笑自己,本题正确。

❹ F 由最后一段医生说的话可知,戴眼镜有助于防止视力恶化,而不是很酷,本题错误。

⑤ T 由最后一段医生说的话可知，有些人不戴眼镜甚至可能会失明，本题正确。

Passage 4 阅读短文，判断句子正（T）误（F）。

> You go to the hospital if you are ill. You may think it is little scary to go to hospital. But doctors and nurses in the hospital can help you feel better. What happens inside hospital? How do the doctors treat patients? Kids learn more about hospitals and doctors at the Teddy Bear Hospital.
>
> Teddy Bear Hospital is in Berlin, Germany. Kids can be doctors here. Their teddy bears are their patients. Real doctors teach the kids a lot. Kids learn to take care of patients.

词汇积累	scary /'skeəri/ *adj.* 恐怖的，吓人的	happen /'hæpən/ *v.* 发生
	treat /tri:t/ *v.* 医治，治疗	patient /'peɪʃnt/ *n.* 病人
	Berlin /bɜː'lɪn/ *n.* 柏林	Germany /'dʒɜːməni/ *n.* 德国

(   ) ❶ Doctors will not help you feel better in the hospital.

(   ) ❷ Teddy Bear Hospital let kids learn about hospitals.

(   ) ❸ There is a Teddy Bear Hospital in China.

(   ) ❹ Kids are the doctors, and their teddy bears are the patients.

(   ) ❺ Kids learn to look after the patients in Teddy Bear Hospital.

 知识要点

take care of表示"照顾，照料"，例如：We need to take care of our bodies.（我们需要照顾好自己的身体。）He's old enough to take care of himself.（他已经不小了，能照顾自己了。）

 参考译文

如果你生病了，就要去医院。你可能会认为去医院有点吓人。但是医院的医生和护士可以帮助你感觉好一些。医院里会发生什么？医生如何治疗病人？孩子们在泰迪熊医院能够了解更多与医院和医生相关的信息。

泰迪熊医院在德国柏林。孩子们可以在这里当医生。他们的玩具熊是他们的病人。真正的医生教给孩子很多东西。孩子们会学着照顾病人。

 答案与解析

❶ F 由第一段第三句可知本题错误。

❷ T 由第一段最后一句可知本题正确。

❸ F 由第二段第一句可知，泰迪熊医院在德国柏林，文中并没有提到中国是否有，本题错误。

❹ T 由第二段第二句和第三句可知本题正确。

❺ T 由第二段最后一句可知，孩子们会在泰迪熊医院学着照顾病人，本题正确。

Passage 5 阅读短文，回答问题。

Last winter, I had a bad cold. I could hardly breathe through my nose. In the morning, my mother brought me a little red teapot. "Tea? I don't like tea!" I said. "I know," Mom said, "but tea is one of the best things you can drink. It's very healthy. This is a special tea when you are sick." There was no way out. I brought the cup to my lips and took a small sip. The tea was strong and bitter. I knew my mom was trying to help me. So I took another sip. Within a few hours, I could breathe through my nose again!

词汇 积累	breathe /briːð/ v. 呼吸	teapot /'tiːpɒt/ n. 茶壶
	special /'speʃ(ə)l/ adj. 专门的，特别的	sick /sɪk/ adj. 生病的
	lip /lɪp/ n. 嘴唇	sip /sɪp/ n. 一小口

❶ What happened last winter?

_____

❷ What did mom bring to me?

_____

❸ Why did mom bring tea to me?

_____

❹ How did the tea taste?

_____

❺ How did I feel after drinking the tea?

_____

知识要点

"one of+the+形容词最高级+名词复数"表示"……是……中最……之一",谓语要用单数形式。例如:Shanghai is one of the biggest cities in the world.(上海是世界上最大的城市之一。)One of the most important languages is English.(最重要的语言之一是英语。)

参考译文

去年冬天,我得了重感冒。我几乎不能用鼻子呼吸。早上,妈妈给我拿来了一个红色的小茶壶。"茶?我不喜欢茶!"我说。"我知道,"妈妈说,"但是茶是你能喝的最好的东西之一。它很健康。这是一种专门给生病的人喝的茶。"没有别的办法了,我把杯子端到嘴边,喝了一小口。这茶又浓又苦。我知道妈妈是为了我好,所以我又喝了一小口。几个小时内,我的鼻子又通气了!

答案与解析

1 I had a bad cold. 由第一句可知答案。

2 A little red teapot. 由第三句可知答案。

3 Because tea is one of the best things I can drink./Because it's very healthy. 文中提到妈妈说喝茶对感冒有好处,她给"我"准备的是专门针对感冒的茶。

4 The tea was strong and bitter. 由倒数第四句可知答案。

5 I could breathe through my nose again! 由最后一句可知答案。

 **Passage 6** 阅读短文，判断句子正（T）误（F）。

Our Hands

We use our hands a lot. We can clap with our hands. We can pick up things with our hands. We can play catch with our hands.

Human hands are different from the hands or paws of other animals. Human hands have four fingers and a thumb. A thumb helps us pick up things. Try picking up something without your thumb. It is hard to do!

Hands help us write, hold things, and play games. What else do hands help us do?

词汇积累		
clap /klæp/ v. 鼓掌，拍手		pick up 捡起，拿起
play catch 玩传球游戏		paw /pɔ:/ n.（动物的）爪
finger /'fɪŋɡə(r)/ n. 手指		thumb /θʌm/ n. 大拇指

(　　) ❶ We can use our hands to play catch.

(　　) ❷ Bear hands have four fingers and a thumb.

(　　) ❸ Human hands are just like animals' paws.

(　　) ❹ It's easy to pick up things without a thumb.

(　　) ❺ Hands can help us do many things.

 知识要点

be different from表示"和······不同"，例如：Boys are different from girls.（男孩和女孩不同。）A goat is different from a sheep.（山羊与绵羊不同。）

 参考译文

我们的双手

我们经常会使用我们的双手。我们能够拍手，能够用手捡东西，能够用手玩传球游戏。

人类的手不同于其他动物的手掌或爪子。人类的手有四根手指和一根大拇指。大拇指能够帮助我们拿起物品。试一试不用拇指去拿东西。这非常困难！

手帮助我们书写，拿住物品和玩游戏。手还能够帮助我们干什么呢？

 答案与解析

❶ T 由第一段最后一句可知本题正确。

❷ F 由第二段第一句可知本题错误。此外，根据常识我们也可作出判断，熊掌跟人类的手结构不同。

❸ F 由第二段第一句可知本题错误。

❹ F 由第二段最后两句可知本题错误。

❺ T 结合全文可知，手可以帮助我们做许多事情，本题正确。

Unit 04　休闲活动

  阅读对话，选择最佳答案。

Andy: Wow! The zoo is so big!

Bill: Look! Monkeys!

Andy: Yes, they are funny. How many monkeys do you see?

Bill: I see two.

Andy: A big monkey and a small one.

Bill: I see some pandas, too.

Andy: Really? How many?

Bill: One, two, three, four, five. Five pandas.

词汇积累	zoo /zu:/ *n.* 动物园	monkey /'mʌŋki/ *n.* 猴子
	funny /'fʌni/ *adj.* 有趣的，好笑的	panda /'pændə/ *n.* 熊猫

(　　) ❶ Where are Andy and Bill?

　　A. They are in a park.

　　B. They are in a zoo.

　　C. They are in a pet shop.

　　D. They are in a supermarket（超市）.

(　　) ❷ What animals do they see?

　　A. Bears and Zebras.　　　　B. Elephants and monkeys.

　　C. Tigers and pandas.　　　　D. Monkeys and pandas.

( ) ❸ How many monkeys do they see?

    A. Two.   B. Five.

    C. Seven.   D. Eleven.

( ) ❹ How many pandas do they see?

    A. Two.   B. Five.

    C. Seven.   D. Eleven.

 知识要点

    对可数名词提问用how many，例如：How many people came to the meeting?（多少人来参加了会议？）对不可数名词提问用how much，例如：How much water do you need?（你要多少水？）

 参考译文

安迪：哇！这个动物园真大啊！

比尔：看！猴子！

安迪：是的，它们真有趣。你看见了多少只猴子？

比尔：我看见了两只。

安迪：一只大猴子和一只小猴子。

比尔：我还看见了一些熊猫。

安迪：真的吗？有几只？

比尔：一、二、三、四、五，有五只熊猫。

 答案与解析

❶ B   由对话第一句可知两人在动物园，B正确。

❷ D   由对话可知，两人看见了猴子和熊猫，D正确。

❸ A   由对话可知，两人在动物园看见了两只猴子，A正确。

❹ B   由对话可知，两人在动物园看见了五只熊猫，B正确。

Passage 2 阅读短文，选择最佳答案。

Today is Sunday. I'm in the park. The park is big and clean. There is an aviary in the park. There are many birds in the aviary. There is a plant house beside the aviary. There are some little trees, much grass and some flowers in the plant house. And I can see a pond near the plant house. There are three ducks in it. And there is a playground behind the pond. Many children are playing in the playground. Some boys are playing football. Some girls are flying kites. I am drawing a picture of the park. I am happy.

词汇 积累	clean /kliːn/ *adj.* 干净的	aviary /ˈeɪvɪərɪ/ *n.* 鸟舍
	beside /bɪˈsaɪd/ *prep.* 在……旁边	pond /pɒnd/ *n.* 池塘

(　　) ❶ The park is _____ .

      A. small but clean　　　　　　　　B. big and clean

      C. small and dirty　　　　　　　　D. big and dirty

(　　) ❷ According to the passage, an aviary is a home for _____ .

      A. dogs　　　　　　　　　　　　B. cats

      C. rabbits　　　　　　　　　　　D. birds

(　　) ❸ The pond is near the _____ .

      A. aviary　　　　　　　　　　　B. plant house

      C. playground　　　　　　　　　D. park

(　　) ❹ Which of the following cannot be found in the plant house?

      A. Flowers.　　　　　　　　　　B. Trees.

C. Grass.   D. Fish.

(   ) ⑤ In the playground, _____.

　　A. some boys are playing football

　　B. some girls are playing hide and seek

　　C. three ducks are walking around

　　D. a dog is running

知识要点

　　beside和near都表示"靠近，在……旁边"，但beside所指的两者之间距离要比near两者之间的距离小得多。例如：Come and sit beside us.（过来坐我们旁边。）They live near Beijing.（他们住得离北京很近。）

参考译文

　　今天是星期天。我在公园里。公园又大又干净。公园里有一个鸟舍。鸟舍里有许多鸟。在鸟舍旁边有一个植物房。在植物房里有一些小树，许多草和一些花。我可以看到植物房附近有一个池塘，里面有三只鸭子。池塘旁边有一个操场。许多孩子在操场上玩。一些男孩在踢足球。一些女孩在放风筝。我正在画一幅公园的画。我很高兴。

答案与解析

❶ B　由第三句 "The park is big and clean." 可知选B。

❷ D　由第五句 "There are many birds in the aviary." 可推断出选D。

❸ B　由第八句 "And I can see a pond near the plant house." 可知选B。

❹ D　由第七句 "There are some little trees, much grass and some flowers in

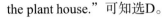
the plant house." 可知选D。

⑤ A 由文中围绕操场的描述可知选A。女孩在操场上放风筝，B错误；鸭子是在池塘里，C错误；D文中并未提及。

 Passage 阅读短文，判断句子正（T）误（F）。

Ping Pong

Have you heard of table tennis? You may also know it as ping pong! In ping pong, two or four players hit a light ball back and forth on a table. They use small paddles. It looks like a smaller version（版本）of tennis. Everyone can play this sport, including（包括）children and adults.

Ping pong is a very popular sport in China. Many Chinese parks and schools have ping pong tables. Chinese players have the most Olympic medals for ping pong. Almost 10 million Chinese people play ping pong in competitions!

Have you played ping pong?

词汇积累	hit /hɪt/ v. 打，击	light /laɪt/ adj. 轻的
	back and forth 来回地	paddle /ˈpæd(ə)l/ n. 球拍
	tennis /ˈtenɪs/ n. 网球	adult /ˈædʌlt/ n. 成年人
	medal /ˈmed(ə)l/ n. 奖牌	competition /ˌkɒmpəˈtɪʃn/ n. 比赛

Unit 04 休闲活动

( ) ① Ping pong is also called table tennis.

( ) ② Players use a big ball on a table.

( ) ③ Only children can play ping pong.

( ) ④ Many people play ping pong in China.

( ) ⑤ Chinese players have the most Olympic medals for ping pong.

 知识要点

　　hear of 表示"听说，听说过"，只强调听说这件事，不强调听说的内容。例如：I hear of the famous Chinese ping pong player Deng Yaping.（我听说过中国著名的乒乓球运动员邓亚萍。）I'm sorry to hear of your serious illness.（得知你病重，我很难过。）

 参考译文

乒乓球

　　你听说过桌上网球吗？你可能也知道它叫乒乓球！在乒乓球比赛中，两名或四名选手在桌上来回击打一个轻球。他们使用小拍子。它看起来就像缩小版的网球。每个人都可以玩这项运动，包括儿童和成年人。

　　乒乓球在中国是一项很受欢迎的运动。中国的许多公园和学校都有乒乓球台。中国运动员拥有最多的乒乓球奥运奖牌。近一千万中国人参加乒乓球比赛！

　　你打过乒乓球吗？

 答案与解析

　　① T　由第一段前两句可知本题正确。

　　② F　由第一段第三句可知，乒乓球使用的是轻球，没有提及大小，但根据生活常识我们知道乒乓球是一个体积很小的球，本题错误。

222222222222049

❸ F   由第一段最后一句可知本题错误。

❹ T   由第二段第一句可知本题正确。

❺ T   由第二段第三句可知本题正确。

 Passage 4 阅读短文，判断句子正（T）误（F）。

Dear friend,

My name is Peter. I am 11 years old. I am in Grade 3 at Guangming School. My favourite subject is P.E. I have P.E. classes on Wednesday and Friday. We have a nice, big playground.

I like playing basketball. Today, I am going to play basketball after school. Do you like basketball, too?

Yours,

Peter

( ) ❶ Peter is in Grade 3 at Guangming School.

( ) ❷ Peter's favourite subject is P.E.

( ) ❸ Peter has math classes on Tuesday and Friday.

( ) ❹ There is a nice, small playground in Guangming School.

( ) ❺ Peter likes playing baseball（棒球）.

知识要点

　　like doing sth.表示"喜欢做某事"，可用于描述自己的兴趣爱好。例如：I like watching TV.（我喜欢看电视。）Do you like singing?（你喜欢唱歌吗?）

 参考译文

亲爱的朋友：

　　我的名字叫彼得。我11岁了。我在光明学校三年级。我最喜欢的课是体育课。我每周三和周五都会上体育课。我们有一个很漂亮、很大的操场。

　　我喜欢打篮球。今天放学之后我要去打篮球。你也喜欢篮球吗?

你的朋友

彼得

 答案与解析

❶ F　由第一段第三句可知，彼得在三年级，不是在二年级，本题错误。

❷ T　由第一段第四句可知本题正确。

❸ F　文中并未提及与数学课相关的内容，本题错误。

❹ F　由第一段最后一句可知，操场很大，本题错误。

❺ F　由第二段第一句可知，彼得喜欢的是篮球而不是棒球，本题错误。

Passage 5 阅读短文，回答问题。

Maybe you think cats and dogs don't get along（相处）well. Wrong! This summer, cats and dogs will work together! Kitty Galore is a cat. She is an agent（特工）of a cat spy organization（间谍组织）. She wants to take over（统治）the world. She has a plan. She has to control humans（人类）and dogs first. One night, she dresses up as（乔装打扮成）a dog to steal a classified document（保密文件）from the dogs. The dogs find out Kitty's plan. They decide to stop Kitty and save humans. At the same time, they get help from other cats. Dogs and cats become partners. They will work together to stop Kitty. Will they stop her in time? Find out in the new movie *Cats&Dogs: the Revenge of Kitty Galore*（《猫狗大战之猫怪的复仇》）this summer.

词汇积累		
plan /plæn/ *n.* 计划		control /kən'trəʊl/ *v.* 控制
steal /sti:l/ *v.* 偷		decide /dɪ'saɪd/ *v.* 决定
save /seɪv/ *v.* 解救		partner /'pɑːtnə/ *n.* 伙伴，搭档

1 What does Kitty Galore want to do?

_____

2 Why does Kitty need to dress up as a dog?

_____

3 Who find out Kitty's plan?

_____

④ When can you watch the movie?

_____

⑤ What's the name of the movie?

_____

 知识要点

　　find out表示"找出，发现，查明"，多指通过调查、寻问、打听、研究之后"搞清楚，弄明白"，通常含有"经过困难曲折"的含义，指找出较难找到的、无形的、抽象的东西。例如：Please find out when the train leaves.（请查一下火车什么时候离站。）find表示"找到，发现"，通常指找到或发现具体的东西，也可指偶然发现某物或某种情况，强调的是找的结果。例如：Will you find me a pen?（你替我找支钢笔好吗？）

 参考译文

　　也许你认为猫和狗相处不好。错了！今年夏天，猫和狗将一起工作！基蒂·加洛尔是一只猫。她是一个猫间谍组织的特工。她想要统治世界。她有个计划，必须先控制人类和狗。一天晚上，她装扮成一只狗，想从狗那里偷一份机密文件。小狗们发现了基蒂的计划，他们决定阻止基蒂，拯救人类。同时，他们得到其他猫的帮助。狗和猫成为伙伴，他们将一起阻止基蒂。他们会及时阻止她吗？在今年夏天的新片《猫狗大战之猫怪的复仇》中，你将会找到答案。

 答案与解析

❶ She wants to take over the world.　由第六句可知答案。

❷ Because she wants to steal a classified document from the dogs.　由第九句

中的 "to" 可知，基蒂乔装打扮成狗的目的。

③ The dogs.　由第十句可知答案。

④ This summer.　文章开头和结尾都提到了可以看这部电影的时间。

⑤ *Cats&Dogs: the Revenge of Kitty Galore.*　由最后一句可知答案。

 Passage 6 阅读短文，回答问题。

I'm going to see a movie with my friends this weekend. We love seeing movies, but we all like different kinds. I like to see thrillers and science fictions, my friend Sam loves action movies and comedies and my best friend, Lee, loves a good romance. Because we like different kinds of movies, it can be difficult to choose one to see. So we usually take turns to choose the movie. It's my turn to choose this weekend, so we're going to see *Harry Potter*, a new movie. It's No.1 at the box office, and everyone is saying what a great movie it is. I can't wait!

词汇 积累	weekend /ˌwiːkˈend/ *n.* 周末	thriller /ˈθrɪlə(r)/ *n.* 惊悚片
	fiction /ˈfɪkʃn/ *n.* 虚构	action /ˈækʃn/ *n.* 行动，活动
	comedy /ˈkɒmədi/ *n.* 喜剧	romance /rəʊˈmæns/ *n.* 浪漫（电影）
	choose /tʃuːz/ *v.* 选择，挑选	box office 票房

① What are they going to do this weekend?

_____

 What kinds of movie does Sam like?

_____

③ How do they choose movies?

_____

④ What movie are they going to watch this weekend?

_____

 Is *Harry Potter* a popular movie? Why?

_____

知识要点

   take turns to do sth. 表示"轮流做某事"，例如：We take turns to clean the room.（我们轮流打扫房间。）Try to take turns to ask questions.（试着轮流提问。）

参考译文

   这个周末我要和朋友们去看电影。我们喜欢看电影，但我们都喜欢不同的类型。我喜欢看惊悚片和科幻片，我的朋友萨姆喜欢动作片和喜剧，而我最好的朋友李喜欢浪漫片。因为我们喜欢不同类型的电影，所以很难在选择电影时达成共识。所以我们通常轮流选电影。这个周末轮到我选了，所以我们要去看一部新电影《哈利·波特》。它的票房排名第一，每个人都在说这是一部特别棒的电影。我等不及了！

 答案与解析

① See a movie.　由第一句可知答案。

② Sam loves action movies and comedies.　由第三句可知答案。

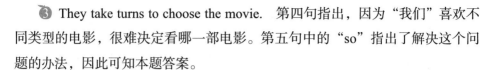

③ They take turns to choose the movie.　第四句指出，因为"我们"喜欢不同类型的电影，很难决定看哪一部电影。第五句中的"so"指出了解决这个问题的办法，因此可知本题答案。

④ *Harry Potter.*　由倒数第三句可知答案。

⑤ Yes. Because it's No.1 at the box office, and everyone is saying what a great movie it is.　由倒数第二句可知答案。

 Passage 7　阅读短文，选择最佳答案。

American boys and girls love to watch television. Some children spend six hours a day in school and four to six hours a day in front of the television. Some even watch television for eight hours or more on Saturday.

Televisions are like books or films. A child can learn good things and bad things from them. Some programs help children to understand the news, and others show people and places from other countries or other time in history. With television, a child does not have to go to the zoo to see animals or to the ocean to see a ship. Boys and girls can see a play or a game at home.

Television brings many places and things into our homes. Some programs show crime (and other things that are bad for children), so parents sometimes help children to find other interesting things to do.

词汇积累	
television /ˈtelɪvɪʒn/ *n.* 电视机	spend /spend/ *v.* 花（时间）
program /ˈprəʊɡræm/ *n.* 节目	understand /ˌʌndəˈstænd/ *v.* 理解
place /pleɪs/ *n.* 地方	crime /kraɪm/ *n.* 犯罪活动

(　　) ❶ How much time a day do American children spend in school?

　　A. They spend five hours a day in school.

　　B. They spend six hours a day in school.

　　C. They spend seven hours a day in school.

　　D. They spend eight hours a day in school.

(　　) ❷ What do American children get from television?

　　A. They can learn bad and good things.

　　B. They can understand the news.

　　C. They can know people and places from other countries.

　　D. All the above are right.

(　　) ❸ What is the bad part of television?

　　A. Television brings many places and events into our homes.

　　B. Boys and girls can see a play, a concert, or a game at home.

　　C. Some programs help children to understand the news.

　　D. Some programs show crime.

(　　) ❹ What can parents do to help children with television?

　　A. Parents can help children to find more interesting things to do.

　　B. Parents can throw away the television.

　　C. Parents can buy a dog for children.

　　D. Parents can hit children.

(　　) ❺ What is the best title of this passage?

　　A. American Children and Television

　　B. Television Is Bad

　　C. Help the Children with Television

　　D. Parents and Television

Part 1 主题阅读

知识要点

some..., and others...表示"有一些……，另外一些……"，and前面的逗号，可以加，也可以不加。例如：Some apples are red, and others are green. （有一些苹果是红的，另外一些是绿色的。）Some people came by car and others came on foot. （有一些人是坐车来的，另外一些人是走路来的。）

参考译文

　　美国男孩和女孩都喜欢看电视。有些孩子每天在学校待六个小时，另外会花四到六个小时坐在电视机前面。有些孩子甚至会在周六看八个或八个小时以上的电视。

　　电视就像书或电影一样。孩子能从电视中学到好的东西，也能学到坏的东西。有些节目帮助孩子们理解新闻，还有些节目展示了来自其他国家或者历史时期的人和地方。通过电视，孩子不用去动物园看动物，也不用去大海上看轮船。男孩和女孩能够在家里看戏剧或者比赛。

　　电视将很多地方和事件带入了我们的家中。有些节目展示了犯罪活动（还有其他对孩子有害的事物），所以父母有时帮助孩子去做一些其他有意思的事情。

答案与解析

❶ B　由第一段第二句可知选B。

❷ D　由第二段可知，A、B、C内容都正确，所以本题选D。

❸ D　由第三段第二句可知选D。

❹ A　由第三段第二句可知选A。

⑤ A 　本文主要介绍了美国儿童观看电视的现状，A符合大意。本文不是讲述父母和电视之间的关系，D错误；文中没有特别说明要帮助儿童应对电视，C错误；电视对于儿童来说有利也有害，B错误。

 Passage 阅读短文，选择最佳答案。

We were on vacation for one week. We packed our bags and went on an airplane. We stayed in a hotel. On Monday, we went to the beach and made a big sandcastle. We splashed in the ocean and then ate some ice cream. On Tuesday, we went to a theme park（主题公园）and watched a parade. On Wednesday, we went to a dinosaur museum（恐龙博物馆）. On Thursday, we went for a walk and looked for bugs. We had a picnic in the park. On Friday, we went up a mountain. On Saturday, we saw rockets at a space center. On Sunday, we went home. What do you like to do on vacation?

词汇积累	vacation /vəˈkeɪʃn/	sandcastle /ˈsændkɑːsl/
	n. 假期	*n.* 沙滩城堡
	splash /splæʃ/	parade /pəˈreɪd/
	v. （在水中）溅着水花行走	*n.* 游行
	bug /bʌg/ *n.* 小昆虫，虫子	picnic /ˈpɪknɪk/ *n.* 野餐
	rocket /ˈrɒkɪt/ *n.* 火箭	space center 太空中心

( ) ❶ How long was this vacation?

A. Two weeks.   B. One week.

C. Three weeks.   D. Four weeks.

( ) ❷ How did they go?

A. They went by train.   B. They went by bus.

C. They went by plane.   D. They went by car.

( ) ❸ Where did they go on Wednesday?

A. They went to a dinosaur museum.

B. They went to the beach.

C. They went up a mountain.

D. They saw rockets at a space center.

( ) ❹ Where did they have some ice cream?

A. In the park.   B. On the mountain.

C. In the space center.   D. On the beach.

( ) ❺ How many places did they go?

A. Five.   B. Six.

C. Four.   D. Seven.

 知识要点

look for表示"寻找"，强调动作和过程。例如：He is looking for the key.（他在找钥匙。）I am looking for my dog.（我正在找我的狗。）

 参考译文

我们有一个为期一周的假期。我们打包行李坐飞机出发了。我们住在酒店。星期一，我们去了海边，在沙滩上堆了一个很大的城堡，并在海里戏水，然后吃了一些冰激凌。星期二，我们去主题公园观看游行。星期

Unit 04 休闲活动

三，我们去了恐龙博物馆。星期四，我们去散步，寻找昆虫，在公园里野餐。星期五，我们爬了山。星期六，我们去太空中心看火箭。星期日，我们回家了。你们假期的时候喜欢做什么呢？

 答案与解析

1 B 由第一句可知，这个假期时长一周，B正确。

2 C 由第二句可知，"我们"乘坐飞机出发，C正确。

3 A 由文中的时间线索可知，"我们"周三去了恐龙博物馆，A正确。

4 D 将题干中的"some ice cream"定位到第五句，D正确。

5 B 由文中的时间线索可知，周一至周六，"我们"每天去不同的地方，周日回家，B正确。

 Passage 9 阅读短文，判断句子正（T）误（F）。

It was my birthday. My whole family went horseback riding. It's easy for us because we live on a farm in the countryside.

That night, we sat around a campfire（营火）and looked at the stars.

My mother brought out a cake with candles on it. "Make a wish." she said. I wished for my own horse.

Just as I blew out the candle, a bright light filled the sky. It was a shooting star（流星）. It soared across the sky.

My mom said a shooting star was a very small rock. It moved

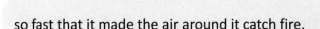

so fast that it made the air around it catch fire.

I was sure she was right, but I thought it was a sign that my wish would come true. If it did, I thought I would name my horse Star.

词汇 积累	whole /həʊl/ *adj.* 全部的	horseback riding 骑马
	countryside /ˈkʌntrisaɪd/ *n.* 乡下	candle /ˈkændl/ *n.* 蜡烛
	blow /bləʊ/ *v.* 吹	fill /fɪl/ *v.* 使充满
	soar /sɔː(r)/ *v.* 高飞	sign /saɪn/ *n.* 迹象

(   ) ❶ We went horseback riding on my father's birthday.

(   ) ❷ I wished for a new bike.

(   ) ❸ A shooting star soared across the sky just as I blew out the candle.

(   ) ❹ The shooting star was a sign that my wish would come true.

(   ) ❺ I wanted to name my own horse Shooting Star.

 知识要点

wish作名词表示"愿望"，例如：The prince's wish came true.（王子的愿望实现了。）wish作动词表示"希望"，例如：I wished for my own watch.（我希望有自己的手表。）

参考译文

那天是我的生日。我们全家去骑马了。这对我们来说很容易，因为我们住在乡下的农场。

那天晚上，我们围坐在营火旁看星星。

妈妈拿出一个插着蜡烛的蛋糕。"许个愿吧！"她说。我希望有自己的马。

就在我吹灭蜡烛的时候，天空中出现了一道亮光。那是一颗流星。它在天空中高高飞过。

妈妈说流星是一块很小的石头。它移动得如此之快，以至于与周围的大气层（摩擦产生高温）而燃烧。

我确信她是对的，但我认为这是我的愿望会实现的象征。如果能实现的话，我想我会给我的马取名为Star。

 答案与解析

❶ F　由第一段前两句可知，是在"我"的生日这一天，全家去骑马，本题错误。

❷ F　由第三段最后一句可知，"我"希望能得到一匹马，本题错误。

❸ T　由第四段可知本题正确。

❹ T　由最后一段第一句可知，"我"认为流星的出现是愿望能够实现的象征，本题正确。

❺ F　由最后一段最后一句可知，"我"想要给马命名为Star，而不是Shooting Star，本题错误。

Passage 10 阅读对话，判断句子正（T）误（F）。

Mike is making a phone call.

Mike: Hello! May I speak to Tom?

Mum: Hold on, please. Tom, it is your phone call.

Tom: Hello, who is that?

Mike: It is Mike, Tom. What are you doing?

Tom: I am watching TV. How about you?

Mike: I am playing a computer game.

Tom: Is it fun?

Mike: Of course. Would you come to my home this afternoon
and play with me?

Tom: All right. See you at three o'clock.

Mike: See you.

词汇
积累 | phone call 电话   hold on （电话用语）别挂断
     | watch /wɒtʃ/ v. 观看   computer game 电脑游戏

( ) ❶ Tom is making a phone call.

( ) ❷ Tom is watching TV.

( ) ❸ Mike is playing football.

( ) ❹ The computer game is not fun.

( ) ❺ Tom and Mike will meet at three o'clock.

 知识要点

Would you...? 在英语中是比较委婉地提出建议或者请求的方式，表示"你要不要……? "。例如：Would you take out the trash? （你可以把垃圾带出去吗? ）Would you like something to eat? （你想吃点什么吗? ）

 参考译文

迈克正在打电话。

迈克：你好！我可以和汤姆说话吗?

妈妈：请稍等。汤姆，有你的电话。

汤姆：你好，请问是哪位?

迈克：汤姆，我是迈克。你在做什么?

汤姆：我在看电视。你呢?

迈克：我在玩电脑游戏。

汤姆：好玩吗?

麦克：当然。你今天下午能来我家和我一起玩吗?

汤姆：好的。三点钟见。

迈克：到时候见。

 答案与解析

❶ F　由对话背景介绍可知，迈克正在打电话，不是汤姆，本题错误。

❷ T　由汤姆的回答可知，他正在看电视，本题正确。

❸ F　由迈克的回答可知，他正在玩电脑游戏，而不是在踢足球，本题错误。

❹ F　汤姆询问游戏是否有趣，迈克予以肯定，说明电脑游戏好玩，本题错误。

❺ T　由通话内容可知，汤姆和迈克约在三点见面，本题正确。

Unit 05   节日与文化

 Passage 1 阅读短文，回答问题。

Chinese children and American children have different holidays. Mid-Autumn Day（中秋节）and Chinese New Year are Chinese holidays. We have mooncakes and see the moon on the Mid-Autumn Day. Chinese New Year is in January or February.

Halloween, Thanksgiving, Christmas are western（西方的）holidays. Children play trick or treat on Halloween in October. They have turkey and say "Thank you!" on Thanksgiving in November. Christmas is on December 25th. Santa comes with gifts for children.

词汇积累	mooncake /'mu:nkeɪk/ n. 月饼	turkey /'tɜ:ki/ n. 火鸡

❶ Which country celebrates Mid-Autumn Day?

_____

❷ What do people eat on Mid-Autumn Day?

_____

❸ What western festivals are mentioned in this passage?

_____

④ What do children do on Halloween?

_____

⑤ When is Christmas?

_____

 知识要点

　　"在某月"介词用in，例如：in May（在5月），in August（在8月）。"在具体的某一天、某个节日"介词用on，例如：on April 16th, 2020（在2020年4月16日），on Sunday（在星期日），on Mid-Autumn Day（在中秋节）。

 参考译文

　　中国儿童和美国儿童有不同的节日。中秋节和中国新年是中国的节日。我们在中秋节吃月饼，看月亮。中国新年在1月或2月。

　　万圣节、感恩节、圣诞节是西方的节日。孩子们在10月的万圣节玩"不给糖就捣蛋"的游戏。在每年11月的感恩节，人们吃火鸡并说"谢谢你！"。圣诞节在12月25日。圣诞老人带来给孩子们的礼物。

 答案与解析

① China.　由第一段第二句可知，中秋节是中国的节日。

② Mooncakes.　由第一段第三句可知答案。

③ Halloween, Thanksgiving and Christmas.　由第二段第一句可知答案。

④ Children play trick or treat on Halloween.　由第二段第二句可知答案。

⑤ It is on December 25th.　由第二段倒数第二句可知答案。

Part 1 主题阅读

 Passage 2 阅读短文，选择最佳答案。

March 12th is Tree-Planting Day. Do you know what can we do on this day? Many people go out to plant trees. They plant trees on the hills, in the parks or along the roads. First, they dig holes, then put the young trees into the holes and put the earth back. At last, they water the young trees. They know trees are people's friends and will take good care of the trees. The forest is the clothes（衣服）of mother earth. Let us plant trees on Tree-Planting Day!

词汇积累
hill /hɪl/ n. 山丘，小山
hole /həʊl/ n. 洞；孔；坑
dig /dɪg/ v. 挖（土）；凿（洞）
forest /'fɒrɪst/ n. 森林

（　）**1** When is Trees-Planting Day?

A. It is on March 13th.   B. It is on April 12th.

C. It is on March 12th.   D. It is on March 14th.

（　）**2** What can we do on Tree-Planting Day?

A. We can cut down trees.

B. We can plant trees.

C. We can buy some trees.

D. We can put the old trees into the holes.

（　）**3** What do you know about trees from this passage?

A. Trees are our friends.

B. We should take care of trees.

C. Forest is the clothes of mother earth.

D. All the above are right.

(   ) **4** Why should we plant trees?

    A. Because we should do what others do.

    B. Because our parents ask us to plant trees.

    C. Because it is good for our mother earth.

    D. Because it is our homework.

(   ) **5** How many kinds of things should we do when planting trees?

    A. Three.   B. Four.

    C. Five.   D. Six.

 知识要点

    earth表示"土，泥土"，例如：She put some earth into the pot.（她在花盆里放了一些泥土。）earth还表示"地球"，例如：The earth moves round the sun.（地球围绕太阳旋转。）

 参考译文

    3月12日是植树节。你知道这一天我们能做什么吗？许多人会出门种树。他们在山上、公园里或公路边种树。首先，他们挖坑，然后将树苗插入坑中，将土填回坑里。最后，他们给树苗浇水。他们知道树木是人类的朋友，所以会悉心照料树苗。森林是地球母亲的衣衫。让我们在植树节一起植树吧！

 答案与解析

1 C   由第一句可知选C。根据常识同学们也可作出正确选择。

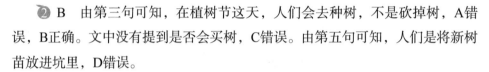
❷ B　由第三句可知，在植树节这天，人们会去种树，不是砍掉树，A错误，B正确。文中没有提到是否会买树，C错误。由第五句可知，人们是将新树苗放进坑里，D错误。

❸ D　由全文可知，A、B、C都正确，所以本题选D。

❹ C　由倒数第二句可知选C。A表示"别人怎么做我们就要怎么做"，这并不是种树的原因。B、D文中并未提及。

❺ A　由第五句和第六句中的"first，then，at last"可知，种树分为三步，A正确。

 Passage 3　阅读短文，判断句子正（T）误（F）。

Today is March 8th. It is Women's Day. We get up early and go to the shop to buy some gifts for our English teacher.

When we come to school, we give our presents and say "Happy Women's Day" to our English teacher. She is very happy. She gets a lot of gifts. There are cards and books.

In the afternoon, all the female teachers need not work. They can have a rest. I am sure they are going to have a good time.

词汇积累	present /'preznt/ *n.* 礼物	gift /gɪft/ *n.* 礼物
	female /'fiːmeɪl/ *adj.* 女的，女性的	rest /rest/ *n.* 休息

(　　) ❶ March 9th is Women's Day.

(　　) ❷ We buy some flowers for our English teacher.

( ) ③ Our English teacher is very happy.

( ) ④ All the female teachers need work in the afternoon.

( ) ⑤ The female teachers are going to have a happy time.

 知识要点

present和gift都表示"礼物"，在现代英语中常可互换使用。例如：birthday presents/gifts（生日礼物）。两者的主要区别在于：gift比present更正式，可指价值较小的礼物，也可指价值相当大的礼物；而present则通常指花费不大的礼物。

 参考译文

今天是3月8日，是妇女节。我们早早就起床去商店买了一些礼物，来送给我们的英语老师。

我们到了学校之后，把礼物送给英语老师，并祝她"妇女节快乐"。她很高兴。她收到很多礼物，有卡片和书。

下午，所有女老师都无须工作。她们可以休息一下。我相信她们会玩得开心。

 答案与解析

① F 由第一段第一句可知，3月8日是妇女节，不是3月9日，本题错误。

② F 由第二段最后两句可知，文中提到的礼物有卡片和书，并没有提到鲜花，本题错误。

③ T 由第二段第二句可知本题正确。

④ F 由第三段第一句可知，女老师妇女节下午不需要工作，本题错误。

⑤ T 由第三段最后一句可知本题正确。

Passage 4 阅读短文，选择最佳答案。

Children's Day is coming. Everyone is so excited. We are going to have a party in the classroom on the first day of June. It begins at seven in the morning and ends at four in the afternoon. Before the party, we are going to do some preparation. Linda is going to bring some snacks and drinks. John is going to bring some balloons because he is going to be a clown. Jessie is going to think of some party games. At the party, children are going to do a lot of things. First, Jessie is going to draw on the blackboard. Next, Linda is going to hang some balloons on the wall. Then, John is going to sing. Finally, we are going to play some games. Come to the party and you will feel happy!

词汇 积累	excited /ɪkˈsaɪtɪd/ *adj.* 感到兴奋的	preparation /prepəˈreɪʃ(ə)n/ *n.* 准备
	snack /snæk/ *n.* 零食	balloon /bəˈluːn/ *n.* 气球
	clown /klaʊn/ *n.* 小丑	hang /hæŋ/ *v.* 悬挂

(　　) ❶ Children's Day is on _____.

　　　　A. the first day of July　　　　　　B. the first day of April

　　　　C. the first day of June　　　　　　D. the first day of May

(　　) ❷ The party will last for _____ hours.

　　　　A. seven　　　　　　　　　　　　B. eight

　　　　C. nine　　　　　　　　　　　　　D. ten

(   ) ❸ _____ is going to be a clown.

       A. Linda   B. John

       C. Jessie   D. Jack

(   ) ❹ Linda is going to hang some _____ on the wall.

       A. pictures   B. snacks

       C. lights   D. balloons

(   ) ❺ Children are not going to _____ at the party.

       A. eat snacks   B. play games

       C. dance   D. have some drinks

 知识要点

    be going to do sth.表示"打算做某事，将要做某事"，多指计划要做的事情，例如：I'm going to take this book to school tomorrow.（我明天打算把这本书带到学校。）I'm going to do my homework this afternoon.（我打算今天下午做家庭作业。）

 参考译文

    儿童节就要到了。每个人都很兴奋。我们将在六月的第一天在教室里举行聚会。早上七点开始，下午四点结束。在聚会之前，我们要做一些准备。琳达打算带一些零食和饮料。约翰要带一些气球，因为他要当小丑。杰西会想出一些聚会游戏。在聚会上，孩子们会做很多事情。首先，杰西要在黑板上画画。接下来，琳达打算把一些气球挂在墙上。然后，约翰要唱歌。最后，我们要玩一些游戏。来参加聚会吧，你会感到很开心的!

 答案与解析

❶ C   由第三句以及生活常识可知选C。

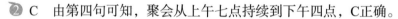
❷ C 由第四句可知，聚会从上午七点持续到下午四点，C正确。

❸ B 由第七句可知选B。

❹ D 由倒数第四句可知选D。

❺ C 由全文可知，孩子们会在聚会上吃零食、喝饮料，还会玩游戏，但是没有提到会跳舞，本题选C。

 Passage 5 阅读短文，回答问题。

I like Christmas; it is just like our Spring Festival.

Maybe the Spring Festival is much more important and interesting than Christmas, but I like Christmas better. Because we can spend time with our friends and classmates during Christmas. When it is snowy, Christmas becomes much more lovely, just like in fairy tales. I can imagine I am in a fairy tale. What a beautiful place! So we can also call Christmas "Snowy Lovely Day".

On Christmas Day, shops are red and green. There are so many Christmas cards, Christmas hats, Christmas dolls and many colourful things. We can give a card or a doll to our friends and say "Merry Christmas".

词汇积累	festival /'festɪvl/ n. 节日	important /ɪm'pɔːtnt/ adj. 重要的
	better /'betə(r)/ adv. 更，较大程度地	fairy tale 童话（故事）
	imagine /ɪ'mædʒɪn/ v. 想象	call /kɔːl/ v. 称呼，把……叫作

❶ What is Christmas like?

_____

❷ Why do the author（作者）like Christmas Day better?

_____

❸ How does Christmas become when it is snowy?

_____

❹ What can we also call Christmas?

_____

❺ What can we say to our friends on Christmas?

_____

 知识要点

　　spend time with 表示"花费时间在……上"。例如：Spend time with your child.（花时间陪伴你的孩子。）Spend time with the people you love.（常和你爱的人在一起。）

 参考译文

我喜欢圣诞节,它就像我们的春节一样。

也许春节比圣诞节更重要,更有趣,但我更喜欢圣诞节。因为我们可以在圣诞节期间与我们的朋友和同学共同度过。下雪时,圣诞节变得更加可爱,就像在童话故事里一样。我想象我就在童话里。多么漂亮的地方啊!因此,我们也可以将圣诞节称为"可爱的下雪天"。

在圣诞节那天,商店是红色和绿色的。有很多圣诞贺卡、圣诞帽、圣诞玩偶和许多五颜六色的东西。我们可以给朋友们卡片或玩偶,然后说"圣诞快乐"。

答案与解析

❶ Christmas is like our Spring Festival. 由第一段可知答案。

❷ Because we can spend time with our friends and classmates during Christmas. 由第二段第二句可知答案。

❸ Christmas becomes much more lovely, just like in fairy tales. 将题干中的"when it is snowy"定位到第二段第三句可知答案。

❹ We can also call Christmas "Snowy Lovely Day". 由第二段最后一句可知答案。

❺ We can say "Merry Christmas". 由第三段最后一句可知答案。

Passage 6 阅读短文，选择最佳答案。

Chinese New Year

Chinese New Year is a big holiday in China. It is also celebrated（庆祝）by some people in the United States.

The date of this holiday changes every year. It is always in the winter, though. It happens usually between January 21 and February 20.

People spend the holiday with their family. They have a big dinner the night before the New Year starts. They eat fish, meat, dumplings and more.

People also wear red around this time. Red is thought to bring good luck.

词汇 积累	holiday /'hɒlədeɪ/ *n.* 节日	date /deɪt/ *n.* 日期
	change /tʃeɪndʒ/ *v.* 改变	happen /'hæpən/ *v.* 发生

(   ) ❶ The date of Chinese New Year is always in _____.

      A. spring   B. summer

      C. autumn   D. winter

(   ) ❷ The big holiday happens usually between _____.

      A. February 21 and March 20

      B. January 10 and January 20

      C. January 21 and February 20

D. December 20 and January 11

( ) ③ People usually spend this holiday with their _____.

    A. friends   B. classmates

    C. family   D. teachers

( ) ④ People eat _____ the night before the New Year starts.

    A. fish   B. meat

    C. dumplings   D. all the above

( ) ⑤ Red is thought to bring _____.

    A. money   B. good luck

    C. good health   D. happiness

知识要点

    between表示"（时间上或空间上）在……之间"，例如：The summer holiday is between July and September.（暑假在7月和9月之间。）I sat down between Jo and Diana.（我在乔和戴安娜中间坐下。）

参考译文

中国新年

    中国新年是中国最重大的节日。一些身处美国的人也会庆祝这个节日。

    这个节日的日期每年都在变化。不过它总是在冬天。它通常在1月21日到2月20日之间。

    人们和家人一起过节。在除夕夜，他们会吃一顿丰盛的晚餐。他们吃鱼、肉、饺子，以及更多的食物。

    这个时候人们也穿红色的衣服。红色被认为能带来好运。

 答案与解析

❶ D 由第二段前两句可知，春节的具体日期每年不固定，经常在冬天，D正确。

❷ C 由第二段最后一句可知选C。

❸ C 由第三段第一句可知选C。

❹ D 由第三段最后一句可知选D。

❺ B 由最后一段最后一句可知选B。

Passage 7 阅读短文，判断句子正（T）误（F）。

Spring Festival is the most important festival in China. My parents cleaned and decorated our house before Spring Festival. We also bought lots of things in the supermarket.

On the eve（前夕）of the Spring Festival, we had a big dinner. After dinner, I put on my new clothes, then my father, my mother and I went to the Flower Fairs. Wow! There were many kinds of flowers in the Flower Fairs. I saw lilies（百合花）, tulips（郁金香）, and peach flowers. How colourful and beautiful they were! We bought some flowers and went home happily. We watched TV until midnight. At twelve o'clock, we cheered to welcome the new year.

| 词汇积累 | decorate /'dekəreɪt/ v. 装饰 | flower fair 花市 |
| | midnight /'mɪdnaɪt/ n. 午夜 | cheer /tʃɪə(r)/ v. 欢呼 |

(　　) ① My parents cleaned and decorated the house after Spring Festival.

(　　) ② We went to the supermarket.

(　　) ③ I put on my new clothes on the eve of the Spring Festival.

(　　) ④ I did not see tulips on the Flower Fairs.

(　　) ⑤ We cheered at eleven o'clock.

 知识要点

　　lots of表示"大量，许多"，通常用于肯定句中。例如：Children need lots of love.（孩子需要很多爱。）There are lots of people in the street.（街上有许多人。）

 参考译文

　　春节是中国最重要的节日。我的父母在春节前打扫并装饰了我们的家。我们还在超市买了很多东西。

　　除夕那天，我们吃了一顿丰盛的晚餐。晚餐后，我穿上了新衣服，然后我和父母去了花市。哇！花市上有很多花。我看到了百合花、郁金香和桃花。它们五颜六色，非常美丽！我们买了一些花后开心地回家了。我们看电视一直看到午夜。12点钟，我们欢呼迎接新年。

 答案与解析

　　① F　由第一段第二句可知，"我"的父母是在春节前打扫并装饰房子的，而不是在春节后，本题错误。

　　② T　由第一段最后一句可知本题正确。

　　③ T　由第二段前两句可知本题正确。

　　④ F　由第二段第五句可知，"我"看到了百合花、郁金香和桃花，本题错误。

　　⑤ F　由第二段最后一句可知，晚上12点，我们欢呼迎接新年，而不是11点，本题错误。

Passage 8 阅读短文，判断句子正（T）误（F）。

Happy Birthday

"Happy birthday to you, happy birthday to you..."

You sing that song many times throughout the year. People around the world sing it in different languages. Some people have birthday cakes and candles too. Some celebrate（庆祝）their birthdays in other ways.

In China, children and their families eat noodles for a long life.

In India, a child gives chocolates to everyone.

In Mexico, a child breaks open（打开）a piñata. Everyone shares the candies inside.

In Russia, a child might have a birthday pie with a birthday wish cut into the crust.

Birthdays are fun around the world!

词汇积累		
throughout /θru:ˈaʊt/ v. 贯穿（整个时期）		language /ˈlæŋgwɪdʒ/ n. 语言
chocolate /ˈtʃɒklət/ n. 巧克力		piñata /pɪˈnjɑːtɑː/ n. 皮纳塔（一种纸糊的容器，内装玩具与糖果）
share /ʃeə(r)/ v. 分享		crust /krʌst/ n. 外壳；表面

( ) ❶ People sing the birthday song on birthdays.

( ) ❷ People around the world celebrate their birthdays in the same way.

( ) ❸ In Mexico, people eat noodles for a long life.

(   ) ④ In India, children give people chocolates.

(   ) ⑤ Children in Russia have a birthday pie on their birthdays.

    give sth. to sb.(= give sb. sth.)表示"给某人某物"，例如：I give the book to my best friend.（我把这本书给我最好的朋友。）Please give me that pencil.（请给我那支铅笔。）

 参考译文

生日快乐

"祝你生日快乐，祝你生日快乐……"

你一整年都在唱这首歌。世界各地的人们用不同的语言唱这首歌。有些人也有生日蛋糕和蜡烛。有些人用其他方式庆祝生日。

在中国，孩子和他们的家人吃面条企盼长寿。

在印度，孩子给每个人巧克力。

在墨西哥，孩子打开皮纳塔。每个人都分享里面的糖果。

在俄罗斯，孩子可能会有一个生日派，把生日愿望切在饼皮上。

世界各地的生日都充满乐趣！

答案与解析

① T   由第一段和第二段第一句可知本题正确。

② F   由第二段最后一句可知，有些人用其他的方式庆祝生日，随后介绍了不同国家庆祝生日的方式，本题错误。

③ F   由第三段可知本题错误。

④ T   由第四段可知本题正确。

⑤ T   由第六段可知本题正确。

Unit 06 我们的动物朋友

Passage 1 阅读短文，回答问题。

There are many kangaroos in Australia. You can see them everywhere outside the cities and towns. Kangaroos have very strong legs, so they are very good at jumping. Their tails are very strong, too. So when they want to have a rest, they rest on their tails. Kangaroos are also very good at taking care of their babies. Mother Kangaroos keep their babies safe in their pockets.

词汇积累	kangaroo /ˌkæŋɡəˈruː/ *n.* 袋鼠	Australia /ɒˈstreɪliə/ *n.* 澳大利亚
	tail /teɪl/ *n.* 尾巴	pocket /ˈpɒkɪt/ *n.* 口袋

① Where can you see many kangaroos outside cities and towns?

_____

② What can kangaroos do with their strong legs?

_____

③ What do kangaroos' tails look like?

_____

④ Where do kangaroos rest?

_____

⑤ Where do mother kangaroos keep their babies?

_____

知识要点

rest表示"休息，小憩"，既可作名词，又可作动词。例如：The doctor told me to have a rest.（医生叫我休息。）You can rest on my bed.（你可以在我床上休息。）

参考译文

澳大利亚有很多袋鼠。在城市和城镇之外，它们随处可见。袋鼠有非常强壮的腿，所以它们非常擅长跳跃。它们的尾巴也很结实。所以当它们想休息的时候，它们就靠在尾巴上休息。袋鼠也很善于照看它们的宝宝。袋鼠妈妈把它们的宝宝放在口袋里确保它们的安全。

答案与解析

❶ In Australia. 由第一句和第二句可知答案。

❷ They can jump very well. 由第三句可知答案，本题大意正确即可。

❸ They are very strong. 由第四句可知答案。

❹ They rest on their tails. 由第五句可知答案。

❺ In their pockets. 由最后一句可知答案。

Passage 2 阅读短文，判断句子正（T）误（F）。

Bug in a Bottle

Charles found a glass bottle. He found the glass bottle in his back yard. It was a pretty glass bottle. It was dark green. He looked inside the dark green bottle. He couldn't see anything. He shook（摇）the bottle. Something came out of the bottle. It landed on the ground. It was a bug. Charles picked up the bug. He looked at it. The bug looked at Charles. Charles put the bottle back on the ground. He put the bug on the ground, next to the bottle. The bug crawled back into the bottle.

词汇 积累	bottle /ˈbɒt(ə)l/ *n.* 瓶子	back yard 后院
	land /lænd/ *v.* 落下	crawl /krɔːl/ *v.* 爬行

(　　) ❶ Charles found a plastic bottle in his back yard.

(　　) ❷ There was nothing in the bottle.

(　　) ❸ Charles dropped the bottle on the ground.

(　　) ❹ Charles filled some water in the bottle.

(　　) ❺ The bug flew away in the end.

知识要点

land作动词表示"降落，落下"，例如：A fly landed on his nose. （一只苍蝇落在他的鼻子上。）land作名词表示"陆地，大地"，例如：The elephant is the largest living land animal. （大象是现存最大的陆地动物。）

 参考译文

瓶子里的小虫

查尔斯发现了一个玻璃瓶。他在后院发现的这个玻璃瓶。这是一个漂亮的玻璃瓶。它是深绿色的。他往深绿色的瓶子里看。他什么也没看到。他摇了摇瓶子。有东西从瓶子里出来了。它掉在了地上。这是一只小虫。查尔斯捡起了小虫。他看了看。小虫也看了看查尔斯。查尔斯把瓶子放回地上。他把虫子放在瓶子旁边的地上。虫子又爬回了瓶子里。

 答案与解析

❶ F　由前两句可知，查尔斯在后院发现了一个玻璃瓶，而不是塑料瓶，本题错误。

❷ F　由第七句和第八句可知中，瓶子里有东西掉出来，本题错误。

❸ F　结合全文，查尔斯没有将瓶子扔在地上，本题错误。

❹ F　结合全文，查尔斯没有往瓶子里注水，本题错误。

❺ F　由最后一句可知，虫子最后爬回瓶子里了，而不是飞走了，本题错误。

Unit 06 我们的动物朋友

 Passage **3**　阅读短文，判断句子正（T）误（F）。

The Forest at Night

When the sun goes down, it is time for bed, right? Not for everyone! Many animals sleep or rest in the nighttime, like we do. But some animals are just waking up! We call these animals nocturnal（夜行的）. That means "awake at night". Nocturnal animals sleep during the day. At night, they eat, move and make noise.

In a forest at night, you might hear owls hooting（鸣叫）. You might hear crickets chirping（唧唧叫）. You could hear a mouse running over dry leaves.

The forest is a busy place at night.

词汇 积累	nighttime /ˈnaɪtˌtaɪm/ n. 夜间	wake up 醒来
	awake /əˈweɪk/ adj. 醒着的	move /muːv/ v. 行动，活动
	owl /aʊl/ n. 猫头鹰	cricket /ˈkrɪkɪt/ n. 蟋蟀

(　　) ❶ Everyone goes to sleep when night comes.

(　　) ❷ Nocturnal animals sleep during the day.

(　　) ❸ Owls might hoot during the day.

(　　) ❹ Crickets might chirp at night.

(　　) ❺ The forest is a quiet place at night.

087

知识要点

hear sb. doing sth.表示"听到某人正在做某事"，常用于现场即时描述。例如：I hear her crying.（我听到她正在哭。）而hear sb. do sth.表示"听到某人做过某事"，多用于回忆性描述。例如：Did you hear them quarrel last night?（你昨晚听到他们吵架了吗？）

参考译文

夜晚的森林

当太阳下山时，我们就该去睡觉了，对吗？并不是所有人都这样！很多动物和我们一样，在夜晚睡觉或休息。但是有一些动物则刚刚醒来！我们称它们为夜行动物，这意味着它们在夜间是醒着的。夜行动物在白天睡觉。到了晚上，它们进食、行动和发出声响。

在夜晚的森林中，你可能会听到猫头鹰鸣叫，你可能会听到蟋蟀在唧唧叫，你可能还会听到老鼠跑过干燥的叶子发出的声响。

夜晚的森林是一个忙碌的地方。

答案与解析

❶ F　由第一段第二句可知，并不是所有的生物都在夜间睡觉，本题错误。

❷ T　由第一段倒数第二句可知本题正确。

❸ F　由第二段第一句可知，猫头鹰鸣叫发生在夜间而不是白天，本题错误。

❹ T　由第二段第二句可知本题正确。

❺ F　由最后一段可知本题错误。

Passage 4 阅读短文，选择最佳答案。

My Dog

I have a dog. Her name is Misty. She loves to play ball.

I throw the ball to Misty. She uses her teeth to pick it up.

Then she runs to me. She drops the ball at my feet.

If Misty hears a noise, she stops. She raises her ears and listens. Misty barks if she sees another dog. She barks loudly to protect me.

After we play ball, we go inside. Misty runs to her bowl and drinks water. I give her some dog food to eat. Then Misty takes a nap.

词汇积累	throw /θrəʊ/ v. 扔，抛	drop /drɒp/ v. 丢下，掉下
	raise /reɪz/ v. 提升，竖起	bark /bɑːk/ v. 狗吠
	protect /prə'tekt/ v. 保护	take a nap 小睡，打盹儿

( ) **1** Misty loves to _____.

　　A. swim　　　　　　　　　B. fly a kite

　　C. play ball　　　　　　　D. run

( ) **2** Misty uses her _____ to pick up the ball.

　　A. hand　　　　　　　　　B. nose

　　C. paw　　　　　　　　　D. teeth

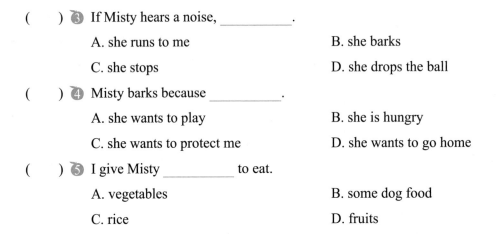

( ) ❸ If Misty hears a noise, _____ .

      A. she runs to me   B. she barks

      C. she stops   D. she drops the ball

( ) ❹ Misty barks because _____ .

      A. she wants to play   B. she is hungry

      C. she wants to protect me   D. she wants to go home

( ) ❺ I give Misty _____ to eat.

      A. vegetables   B. some dog food

      C. rice   D. fruits

  知识要点

    love to do sth.表示"喜爱做某事"，例如：My brother loves to read books.（我哥哥喜欢读书。）I love to swim in the swimming pool.（我喜欢在游泳池里游泳。）

 **参考译文**

我的狗狗

    我有一只狗。她的名字叫米丝蒂。她喜欢玩球。

    我把球扔给米丝蒂。她用牙齿把它捡起来。

    然后她跑向我。她把球丢在我脚边。

    如果米丝蒂听到声音，她就会停下来。她竖起耳朵听。米丝蒂如果看到另一只狗就会叫。她大声吠着保护我。

    玩完球，我们就进屋。米丝蒂跑到她的碗边喝水。我给她一些狗粮吃。然后米丝蒂睡个午觉。

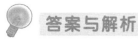

 答案与解析

❶ C　由第一段第三句可知选C。

❷ D　由第二段第二句可知选D。

❸ C　由第四段第一句可知选C。

❹ C　由第四段最后一句可知选C。

❺ B　由最后一段倒数第二句可知选B。

Passage **5** 阅读短文，回答问题。

Jellyfish live in the ocean. They can be clear or can be colours like pink, yellow, or blue. Jellyfish are invertebrates（无脊椎动物）, which means they do not have a backbone. They also do not have a brain, eyes or heart. Their bodies have tentacles（触须）, which they use to sting their prey（猎物）. Jellyfish eat crabs（螃蟹）, fish, plants and other jellyfish. They will also sting people if they touch them, which really hurts!

Jellyfish have to stay away from sea turtles（海龟）, who will try to eat them. Let's learn more about jellyfish!

词汇积累	clear /klɪə(r)/ *adj.* 透明的	mean /miːn/ *v.* 意味着
	backbone /'bæk‚bəʊn/ *n.* 脊椎	sting /stɪŋ/ *v.* 刺；蜇
	touch /tʌtʃ/ *v.* 接触	hurt /hɜːt/ *v.* 使疼痛

1 Where do jellyfish live?

_____

2 What are the colours of jellyfish?

_____

3 Do jellyfish have bones?

_____

4 What do jellyfish use to sting their prey?

_____

5 What do sea turtle eat?

_____

 知识要点

stay away from表示"远离……，回避……"，例如：The doctor tells him to stay away from fat food.（医生叫他不要吃高脂肪的食物。）Stay away from buildings and trees.（远离建筑物和树木。）

 参考译文

水母生活在海洋中。它们是透明的，或是粉色的、黄色的或蓝色的。水母是无脊椎动物，也就是说它们没有脊椎。它们也没有大脑、眼睛和心脏。它们的身体有触角，用来蜇猎物。水母吃螃蟹、鱼、植物和其他水母。如果人类摸了它们，它们也会蜇人，真的很疼！

水母必须远离海龟，海龟会试图吃掉它们。让我们进一步了解水母吧！

Unit 06 我们的动物朋友

答案与解析

① Jellyfish live in the ocean. 由第一段第一句可知答案。

② Pink, yellow, or blue. 由第一段第二句可知答案。

③ No, they don't. 由第一段第三句可知答案。

④ Tentacles. 由第一段第五句可知答案。

⑤ Jellyfish. 由第二段第一句可知答案。

Passage 6 阅读短文，选择最佳答案。

Lions are big animals. They are the second largest cat in the world. They can be over six feet tall and weigh up to 500 pounds. Male lions are often bigger than female lions. Lions have tan or yellowish-brown fur. They have long tails. Lions live in grasslands and woodlands（林地）. They eat big animals like antelopes（羚羊）, zebras, goats, giraffes, and buffaloes（水牛）. They also eat small animals like rabbits, birds, and reptiles（爬行动物）. Lions' predators（捕食者）are hyenas（鬣狗）, leopards and jackals（豺狼）. They are most likely to hunt baby lions.

词汇积累	weigh /weɪ/ v. 有……重	pound /paʊnd/ n. 磅
	male /meɪl/ adj. 雄性的	female /ˈfiːmeɪl/ adj. 雌性的
	tan /tæn/ adj. 棕黄色的	fur /fɜː(r)/ n. 皮毛

093

(　　) ❶ Lions are the _____ in the world.

    A. largest cat   B. largest animal

    C. second largest cat   D. second largest animal

(　　) ❷ Male lions are often _____ than female lions.

    A. taller   B. smaller

    C. bigger   D. shorter

(　　) ❸ Lions don't live in _____.

    A. grasslands   B. woodlands

    C. rainforest   D. zoos

(　　) ❹ Which of the following animals do lions eat?

    A. Giraffes.   B. Turtles.

    C. Monkeys.   D. Frogs.

(　　) ❺ Leopards may hunt _____.

    A. adult lions   B. baby lions

    C. mother lions   D. dead（死亡的）lions

知识要点

　　"the +序数词（不包括first）+形容词最高级+单数名词+in+范围"表示"在某范围内是第几……的"，例如：The yellow river is the second longest river in China.（黄河是中国第二长河。）Tony is only shorter than Jim. He is the second tallest boy in his class.（托尼只比吉姆矮。他是班里第二高的男生。）

参考译文

　　狮子是一种大型动物，它们是世界上第二大猫科动物。它们可以超过6英尺高，重达500磅。雄狮通常比雌狮大。狮子有棕黄色或黄褐色的皮毛。

它们有长长的尾巴。狮子生活在草原和林地。它们吃大型动物，如羚羊、斑马、山羊、长颈鹿和水牛。它们也吃小动物，如兔子、鸟类和爬行动物。狮子的捕食者是鬣狗、豹子和豺狼。它们最有可能捕食幼狮。

 答案与解析

1. C　由第二句可知选C。

2. C　由第四句可知选C。B与原文相反，A和D在文中并未提及。

3. C　由第七句可知，狮子生活在草原和林地，由生活经验可知动物园里也有狮子，本题用排除法，选C。

4. A　由倒数第四句可知选A。

5. B　由最后一句可知选B。

Passage 7 阅读短文，回答问题。

What animals are there in the sea? There are all kinds of animals in the sea. Look! They are coming. This is an octopus. The octopus is spraying ink. This is a shark. The shark has sharp teeth. This is a whale. The whale shoots water into the air. This is a sea turtle. The sea turtle has hard shell. These are starfishes. The starfishes have five legs. These are angelfishes. The angelfishes have beautiful colours. This is a lobster. The lobster has strong claws. This is a jellyfish. The jellyfish has a soft body. They are different. But all of them live in the sea.

词汇积累		
	spray /spreɪ/ v. 喷，喷洒	ink /ɪŋk/ v. 墨汁
	sharp /ʃɑːp/ adj. 锋利的	whale /weɪl/ n. 鲸
	shoot /ʃuːt/ v. 发射	shell /ʃel/ n. 壳
	lobster /ˈlɒbstə(r)/ n. 龙虾	claw /klɔː/ n. 螯，钳

❶ What is the octopus doing?

_____

❷ What does the shark have?

_____

❸ What does the whale do?

_____

❹ How many legs do starfishes have?

_____

⑤ How many kinds of sea animals are mentioned in this passage?

_____

 知识要点

　　hard 在文中作形容词，表示"坚硬的，坚固的"，例如：It is a very hard stone.（这是一块坚硬的宝石。）hard还可以作副词，表示"努力地"，例如：You must try harder.（你得更加努力。）

 参考译文

　　海里有什么动物？海里有各种各样的动物。看！它们来了。这是一条章鱼。章鱼正在喷墨汁。这是一条鲨鱼。鲨鱼的牙齿很锋利。这是一条鲸鱼。鲸鱼将水喷向空中。这是一只海龟。海龟有坚硬的龟壳。这些是海星。海星有五条腿。这些是神仙鱼。神仙鱼颜色美丽。这是龙虾。龙虾有很强壮的钳子。这是水母。水母身体柔软。它们都不一样。但是它们都生活在海里。

 答案与解析

① The octopus is spraying ink.
由第五句和第六句可知答案。

② The shark has sharp teeth.
由第八句可知答案。

③ The whale shoots water into the air.　由第十句可知答案。

④ The starfishes have five legs.　定位到对海星的描述可知答案。

⑤ There are eight kinds of sea animals in this passage./Eight.　全文提到了 "octopus, shark, whale, sea turtle, starfishes, angelfishes, lobster, jellyfish" 共八种海洋动物。

Passage 8 阅读短文，回答问题。

Toucans are tropical birds that live in jungles. They make nests in tree hollows（凹陷处）or holes.

Toucans like to eat fruit, insects, and small lizards（蜥蜴）. They have to stay away from predators（捕食者）like jaguars（美洲豹）, eagles（老鹰）, and hawks（隼）. Toucans are 10 to 30 inches long and weigh less than two pounds. Their bodies are covered in black feathers and their necks are often white or yellow. Toucans have colourful bills that are about eight inches long but are not very heavy or strong.

词汇积累		
	tropical /ˈtrɒpɪk(ə)l/ *adj.* 热带的	jungle /ˈdʒʌŋg(ə)l/ *n.* 丛林
	nest /nest/ *n.* 鸟巢，鸟窝	insect /ˈɪnsekt/ *n.* 昆虫
	inch /ɪntʃ/ *n.* 英寸	cover /ˈkʌvə(r)/ *v.* 覆盖
	feather /ˈfeðə(r)/ *n.* 羽毛	bill /bɪl/ *v.* 鸟嘴

❶ Where do toucans live?

_____

❷ Where do toucans make nests?

_____

❸ What do toucans eat?

_____

❹ What animals eat toucans?

_____

Unit 06 我们的动物朋友

⑤ What colours can you see on toucans' bodies?

_____

知识要点

"be+长度+long" 表示 "有……长"，例如：The snake is one meter long.（这条蛇有1米长。）The bridge is 100 meters long.（这座桥有100米长。）"weigh+重量" 表示 "有……重"，例如：The rabbit weighs 5 kg.（这只兔子重5千克。）It weighs nearly 27 kilos.（它重量接近27公斤）。

参考译文

大嘴鸟是生活在丛林中的热带鸟类，它们在树的凹陷处或树洞里筑巢。

大嘴鸟喜欢吃水果、昆虫和小蜥蜴。它们必须远离像美洲豹、老鹰和隼这样的掠食者。大嘴鸟长10到30英寸，体重不到两磅。它们的身体覆盖着黑色的羽毛，脖子通常是白色或黄色的。大嘴鸟有五颜六色的喙，长约8英寸，但不是很笨重，也不强壮。

答案与解析

① They live in jungles. 由第一段第一句可知答案。

② They make nests in tree hollows or holes. 由第一段第二句可知答案。

③ They eat fruit, insects, and small lizards. 由第二段第一句可知答案。

④ Jaguars, eagles and hawks. 由第二段第二句可知答案。

⑤ Black, white and yellow. 由第二段倒数第二句可知答案。

Unit 07 自然与环境

 Passage 1 阅读短文，判断句子正（T）误（F）。

Facts About Fog

Have you ever stood in fog? Fog can make it hard to see what is around you.

Fog is really just a cloud that forms close to the ground. It is made of drops of water that stick to little bits of dust in the air. Fog can even touch the ground.

Sometimes we see fog above water. That happens when cool air moves over warm water in a lake or in an ocean.

词汇积累		
fog /fɒg/ *n.* 雾		form /fɔːm/ *v.* 形成
drop /drɒp/ *n.* 水珠，水滴		stick to 粘住
dust /dʌst/ *n.* 灰尘，尘埃		above /əˈbʌv/ *prep.* 在……上面

(   ) ❶ You can see things clearly in the fog.

(   ) ❷ Fog is made of bits of dust.

(   ) ❸ Fog is made of drops of water.

(   ) ❹ Fog can touch the ground.

(   ) ❺ Sometimes we can see fog under water.

知识要点

above/on/over都表示"在……上"，区别如下：above指的"上方"范围更广，over指正上方，on指有接触的上方。例如：The plane flies above the clouds.（飞机在云彩上方飞行。）There is a bridge over the river.（河上有座桥。）My schoolbag is on the desk.（我的书包在桌子上。）

 参考译文

雾的真相

你曾经站在雾中吗？雾会让你很难看清周围的事物。

雾实际上只是在接近地面时形成的云。它是由空气中粘有微小尘土的水滴组成的。雾甚至能触及地面。

有时我们看到水面上有雾。当冷空气移动到湖泊或海洋中的温水上方时，就会发生这种情况。

 答案与解析

❶ F 由第一段第二句可知，雾会让你看不清周围的事物，本题错误。

❷ F 由第二段第二句可知，雾是由空中的粘有微小尘土的水滴构成的，而不是小尘土颗粒，本题错误。

❸ F 同第二题的分析，本题错误。

❹ T 由第二段最后一句可知，雾是可以沉到地面的，本题正确。

❺ F 由第三段第一句可知，雾可以浮在水面上，而不是沉在水下，本题错误。

 **Passage 2** 阅读短文，选择最佳答案。

Months of the Year

A calendar shows the days, weeks, and months of a year. You may have a calendar at home. You may have a calendar at school.

Take a close look at a calendar. You will see there are seven days in a week. There are four full weeks in a month. There are 12 months in a year. Can you name all the months in a year?

Some months are 31 days long. Other months are 30 days long. February is the shortest month. Most years February is only 28 days long. Other years February is 29 days long. Years when February is 29 days long are called leap years.

词汇 积累	calendar /'kæləndə(r)/ *n.* 日历	show /ʃəʊ/ *v.* 显示，说明
	full /fʊl/ *adj.* 完整的	leap year 闰年

(　　) ❶ A calendar shows _____.

A. days

B. weeks

C. months of a year

D. days, weeks and months of a year

(　　) ❷ There are _____ in a _____.

A. 30 days; week   B. 7 days; month

C. 30 days; year   D. 7 days; week

(   ) ❸ _____ is the fifth month of a year.

      A. March   B. April

      C. May   D. June

(   ) ❹ _____ is the shortest month of a year.

      A. January   B. February

      C. November   D. December

(   ) ❺ Years when February is 29 days long are called _____.

      A. lucky years   B. special years

      C. new years   D. leap years

 知识要点

    name在文中作动词，表示"说出……的名字"，例如：Can you name five big cities in China?（你能说出中国的五个大城市的名字吗？）Can you name all the American states?（你能说出美国所有的州名吗？）

 参考译文

一年中的月份

    日历显示一年中的日、周和月。你家里可能有日历。你的学校里也可能有日历。

    仔细看看日历。你会看到一星期有7天。一个月有整整4个星期。一年有12个月。你能说出一年中所有的月份吗？

    有些月份长达31天。其他月份是30天。2月是最短的月份。大多数年份的2月只有28天。其他年份的2月是29天。2月有29天的年份叫作闰年。

Part 1 主题阅读

 答案与解析

① D 由第一段第一句可知选D。

② D 由第二段第二、三、四句可知，匹配关系正确的是D。根据常识同学们也可作出正确选择。

③ C 本题考查学生对月份单词的掌握情况，一年中第五个月是"May"，C正确。

④ B 由第三段第三句可知选B。根据常识同学们也可作出正确选择。

⑤ D 由第三段最后一句可知选D。

Passage ③ 阅读短文，选择最佳答案。

The Four Seasons

Some places have four seasons every year. Do you know their names? The seasons are winter, spring, summer, and autumn.

Winter is the coldest time of the year. Spring comes next. Many animals are born in spring. Many new plants grow then too.

Summer is a time of sunshine and hot weather. In autumn, the weather gets cooler. The leaves fall off trees.

Some people call autumn by another name. They call it fall!

词汇积累	grow /ɡrəʊ/ v. 生长	sunshine /'sʌnʃaɪn/ n. 阳光
	weather /'weðə(r)/ n. 天气	cool /kuːl/ adj. 凉爽的
	leaf /liːf/ n. 叶子	fall off 掉落

(   ) ❶ _____ is the coldest season.

         A. Spring   B. Summer

         C. Winter   D. Autumn

(   ) ❷ Many animals are born in _____ .

         A. spring   B. summer

         C. winter   D. autumn

(   ) ❸ _____ is the hottest season.

         A. Spring   B. Summer

         C. Winter   D. Autumn

(   ) ❹ In autumn, _____ .

         A. many new plants grow   B. animals are born

         C. the leaves fall off trees   D. the weather gets warmer

(   ) ❺ _____ is also called fall.

         A. Spring   B. Summer

         C. Winter   D. Autumn

 知识要点

     be born in表示"出生于某时间或地点"，例如：Li Ping was born in 2002.（李平出生于2002年。）Tom was born in Beijing.（汤姆出生于北京。）

 参考译文

四季

     有些地方每年有四个季节。你知道它们的名字吗？这些季节是冬季、春季、夏季和秋季。

     冬季是一年中最冷的时候。春季随后来临。许多动物在春季出生。许多新植物也在那时生长。

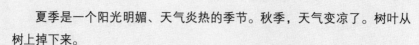

夏季是一个阳光明媚、天气炎热的季节。秋季，天气变凉了。树叶从树上掉下来。

有些人用另一个名字来称呼秋季。他们称之为秋天！

 答案与解析

① C 由第二段第一句可知选C。

② A 由第二段第三句可知选A。

③ B 由第三段前两句可知，夏季是一年中最热的季节，B正确。

④ C 由第三段最后一句可知C正确。A和B是对春季的描述，D与文意相反。

⑤ D 由最后一段可知选D。

 Passage **阅读短文，判断句子正（T）误（F）。**

Why Do We Have Summer?

Summer starts on the longest day of the year. We call that day the summer solstice（夏至）.

Summer days are warm and long. There is more sunlight. People spend more time outdoors.

Why do we have summer? Earth tilts as it travels around the sun. When Earth's northern half leans toward the sun, that part has summer.

Summer starts in the northern half of Earth around June 21. At that time, it is winter in the southern part of Earth. That is because the Earth's southern half is tilted away from the sun.

词汇 积累	sunlight /'sʌnlaɪt/ n. 阳光	tilt /tɪlt/ v. 倾斜
	travel /'trævl/ v. （物体）移动	lean /li:n/ v. 倾斜

(　　) ❶ Summer starts on summer solstice.

(　　) ❷ Summer days are cool and long.

(　　) ❸ People spend more time at home in summer.

(　　) ❹ When Earth's southern half leans toward the sun, that part has summer.

(　　) ❺ Summer starts in the northern half of Earth around July 21.

 知识要点

　　at that time表示"在那时"，例如：At that time, she tells me the truth.（那时她告诉了我真相。）What happened at that time?（那时发生了什么？）

 参考译文

我们为什么有夏天？

夏天是从一年中白天最长的一天开始的。我们称这一天为夏至。

夏天的日子温暖而漫长。夏天有更多的阳光。人们花更多的时间在户外。

我们为什么有夏天呢？地球绕太阳运行时是倾斜的。当地球的北半部向太阳倾斜时，那部分就有了夏天。

夏天在6月21日左右从地球的北半部开始。那时，在地球的南半部是冬天。这是因为地球的南半部远离太阳。

 答案与解析

❶ T   由第一段可知本题正确。

❷ F   由第二段第一句可知，夏天的日子是温暖的，而不是凉爽的，本题错误。

❸ F   由第二段最后一句可知，夏天人们会花更多时间在户外活动，本题错误。

❹ F   由第三段最后一句可知，当北半球向太阳倾斜时将会迎来夏天，而不是题干中所说的南半球，本题错误。

❺ F   由最后一段第一句可知，北半球的夏天始于6月21日左右，而不是题干中所说的7月21日，本题错误。

 Passage 5 阅读短文，选择最佳答案。

From Morning to Night

It is morning. It is time for a new day to begin. The morning sun appears. It slowly brightens the sky.

It is noon. It is the middle of the day. The sun is high in the sky. The sunlight is bright.

It is evening. The sunlight becomes less bright. The sun is moving lower in the sky. The sky may change to a reddish colour.

It is night. The sun is gone from the sky. The sky is dark without sunlight. The moon and the stars shine in the night sky. Tomorrow a new day will begin again.

> **词汇 积累**
> appear /ə'pɪə(r)/ v. 出现，显现   brighten /'braɪt(ə)n/ v. 使变亮
> reddish /'redɪʃ/ adj. 微红的，淡红的   shine /ʃaɪn/ v. 发光；照耀

( ) ❶ In the morning, _____ appears.

  A. the sun   B. the moon

  C. the star   D. the earth

( ) ❷ _____ is the middle of the day.

  A. Morning   B. Noon

  C. Evening   D. Night

( ) ❸ In the evening, the colour of the sky is _____.

  A. bright   B. dark

  C. reddish   D. lunar（微亮的）

( ) ❹ In what time of the day, there is no sunlight?

  A. Morning.   B. Noon.

  C. Evening.   D. Night.

( ) ❺ Which of the following is wrong?

  A. People start a new day in the morning.

  B. The sun is moving lower in the sky in the evening.

  C. The moon and the stars shine in the night sky.

  D. The moon is moving lower in the sky at night.

知识要点

表示世界上独一无二的事物的名词，前面要用定冠词the。例如：We sat in the sun.（我们坐在阳光下。）There was a rainbow in the sky.（天空中有道彩虹。）

 参考译文

从早晨到夜晚

早上到了。新的一天开始了。早晨的太阳出现了。它慢慢地照亮天空。

中午到了。中午是一天的中间时段。太阳高高地挂在天空中。阳光很明亮。

傍晚到了。阳光变得不那么明亮了。太阳在天空中移动得更低了。天空可能会变成浅红色。

晚上到了。太阳从天空中消失了。没有阳光，天空是黑暗的。月亮和星星在夜空中闪烁。明天，新的一天又将开始。

 答案与解析

1 A 由第一段第三句可知选A。

2 B 由第二段前两句可知选B。

3 C 由第三段最后一句可知选C。

4 D 由第四段前三句可知选D。

5 D 结合全文，夜晚月亮应该是逐渐升高，D不符合文意。注意本题要求选错误说法。A、B和C均与原文对应。

 Passage 阅读短文，选择最佳答案。

Some Trees Give Us Food

Trees are plants. They need sun and water to grow. Some trees grow fruits or nuts that people eat.

Apples grow on trees. Apples can be red, yellow, or green. Many people eat apples as a snack.

Oranges grow on trees. They grow in places that have warmer weather. Orange juice comes from oranges.

Coconuts grow on trees. The inside of a coconut has a sweet part that people eat. The coconut is really a very large seed.

Many other foods grow on trees. Cherries, plums, and walnuts （核桃）all come from trees!

词汇积累		
nut /nʌt/ n. 坚果		snack /snæk/ n. 点心，小吃
coconut /'kəʊkəˌnʌt/ n. 椰子		seed /siːd/ n. 种子
plum /plʌm/ n. 李子		walnut /'wɔːlˌnʌt/ n. 核桃

( ) **1** Trees need _____ to grow.

　　　　A. sun and wind　　　　　　　B. salt and water

　　　　C. sun and water　　　　　　　D. sun and salt

( ) **2** Which of the following fruit can be red?

　　　　A. Apple.　　　　　　　　　　B. Banana.

　　　　C. Coconut.　　　　　　　　　D. Orange.

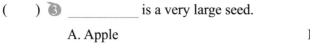

(   ) ❸ _____ is a very large seed.

      A. Apple   B. Orange

      C. Coconut   D. Plum

(   ) ❹ Which of the following is not fruit?

      A. Oranges.   B. Walnuts.

      C. Plums.   D. Cherries.

(   ) ❺ Which of the following do not grow on trees?

      A. Plums.   B. Apples.

      C. Coconuts.   D. Watermelons.

 知识要点

    come from在文中表示"产自，来自"，例如：Much of our butter comes from New Zealand.（我们的黄油大多产自新西兰。）This wool comes from goats, not sheep.（这种羊毛是山羊毛，不是绵羊毛。）

 **参考译文**

果树

    树木是植物。它们需要阳光和水来生长。有些树长出人们可以食用的水果或坚果。

    苹果长在树上。苹果可以是红色、黄色或绿色的。许多人把苹果当零食吃。

    橙子长在树上。它们生长在气候更温暖的地方。橙汁来自橙子。

    椰子长在树上。椰子里面甜的部分可以供人们食用。椰子确实是一个非常大的种子。

    其他许多食物生长在树上。樱桃、李子和核桃都是从树上长出来的！

答案与解析

❶ C 由第一段第二句可知选C。

❷ A 由第二段第二句可知选A。此外，根据常识，香蕉、椰子、橙子不可能是红色的。

❸ C 由第四段最后一句可知选C。

❹ B 橙子、李子、樱桃都是水果，核桃不是水果，B正确。

❺ D 根据全文，李子、苹果、樱桃都长在树上，而根据常识我们知道西瓜长在地上，本题选D。

 Passage **7** 阅读短文，选择最佳答案。

Orange and yellow are bright colours. You can find them just about anywhere.

Stand outside. Look at the street. You might see bright yellow lines. Look around. You might see orange flowers.

Where else can you find these colours? In your kitchen! There might be some orange and yellow foods in your kitchen!

Here is a list of some foods that are orange:

carrots

oranges

pumpkins

Here is a list of some foods that are yellow:

lemons

bananas

corn

What colour is your favourite food?

词汇
积累 line /laɪn/ *n.* 线   carrot /ˈkærət/ *n.* 胡萝卜
      pumpkin /ˈpʌmpkɪn/ *n.* 南瓜   corn /kɔːn/ *n.* 玉米

(　　) ❶ _____ are bright colours.

A. Black and yellow   B. Orange and purple

C. Orange and yellow   D. Brown and yellow

(　　) ❷ According to the passage, you might see some _____ lines on

the street.

A. red   B. green

C. blue   D. yellow

(　　) ❸ Which food is orange?

A. Carrots.   B. Eggs.

C. Cabbages（卷心菜）.   D. Corn.

(　　) ❹ Which food is yellow?

A. Pumpkins.   B. Garlics（大蒜）.

C. Corn.   D. Cherries.

(　　) ❺ Which of the following is wrong?

A. You can find orange and yellow almost everywhere.

B. The colours of traffic lights are red, green and orange.

C. If you look around, there might be some orange flowers.

D. Lemons and bananas can be the same colour.

 知识要点

　　a list of表示"……的清单；一列"，例如：Here is a list of schools in our city.（这是一份我们城市的学校的清单。）There is a list of new books on the table.（桌子上有一列新书目。）

 参考译文

　　橙色和黄色是非常明亮的颜色。你几乎可以在任何地方找到它们。

　　站在外面看这条街，你可能会看到亮黄色的线。环顾四周，你可能会看到橙色的花。

　　你还能在哪里找到这些颜色？在你的厨房里！你的厨房里可能会有一些橙色和黄色的食物！

　　以下是一些橙色食物的清单。

　　胡萝卜

　　橙子

　　南瓜

　　以下是一些黄色食物的清单。

　　柠檬

　　香蕉

　　玉米

　　你最喜欢的食物是什么颜色的？

 答案与解析

　❶ C　由第一段第一句可知选C。

　❷ D　由第二段第三句可知选D。

　❸ A　由文中列举的橙色食物可知选A。根据常识，鸡蛋、卷心菜、玉米都不是橙色的，可以排除。

④ C 由文中列举的黄色食物可知选C。根据常识，南瓜、大蒜、樱桃都不是黄色的，可以排除。

⑤ B 文中并未提及交通信号灯的颜色，但根据常识，我们知道交通信号灯是红、黄、绿三种颜色，B错误。注意本题要求选择错误说法。

 Passage 8 阅读短文，选择最佳答案。

City Life and Country Life

Do you live in a city? A city has many buildings. It also has many roads. It has many cars and lots of noise. Cities are full of people. City life can be full of fun. City life is noisy.

Do you live in the country? The country has lots of grass, trees, and animals. It also has farms. People grow food in the country. Fewer people live in the country than in the city. Country life can be full of fun. Country life is quieter.

词汇积累	building /'bɪldɪŋ/ *n.* 建筑；楼房	road /rəʊd/ *n.* 道路；公路
	noisy /'nɔɪzi/ *adj.* 嘈杂的	quiet /'kwaɪət/ *adj.* 安静的

( ) ❶ City life is _____.

　　A. boring　　　　　　　　　　B. tiring

　　C. quiet　　　　　　　　　　D. full of fun

( ) ❷ _____ has/have many buildings and roads.

　　A. A city

　　B. The country

C. A city and a country

D. Neither a city nor a country

( ) ❸ According to this passage, people grow food in _____.

A. the country   B. cities

C. yards   D. kitchens

( ) ❹ Which of the following is wrong about cities?

A. A city is full of people.

B. A city has many cars.

C. You can hear a lot of noise in a city.

D. Fewer people live in cities than in the country.

( ) ❺ Which of the following is wrong about the country?

A. The country has lots of parks.

B. The country has lots of animals.

C. Country life can be full of fun.

D. Country life is quieter than city life.

 知识要点

　　full of sth.表示"充满……，满是……"，例如：My suitcase was full of books.（我的手提箱装满了书。）She's very lively and full of fun.（她很活泼，挺有趣的。）

 参考译文

城市生活和乡村生活

　　你住在城市里吗？城市有许多建筑物，也有许多道路。城市有很多汽车，噪音很大。城市里到处都是人。城市生活可以充满乐趣。城市生活很嘈杂。

你住在乡村吗？乡村有许多草地、树木和动物。乡村也有农场。人们在乡村种植粮食。住在乡村的人比住在城市的人少。乡村生活可以充满乐趣。乡村生活更安静。

 答案与解析

① D 由第一段倒数第二句可知选D。A、B文中并未提及，C不符文意。

② A 由第一段第二句和第三句可知选A。

③ A 由第二段第四句可知选A。

④ D 由第二段第五句可知，住在乡村的人比住在城市的人少，D不符合对城市的描述。

⑤ A 由第二段可知，B、C、D符合对乡村的描述。A文中并未提及。

Unit 08 幽默故事

A woman walks into a pet shop and sees a cute little dog. She asks the shopkeeper, "Does your dog bite?"

The shopkeeper says, "No, my dog does not bite."

The woman tries to pet the dog and the dog bites her.

"Ouch!" she says, "I thought you said your dog didn't bite!"

The shopkeeper says, "That is not my dog!"

词汇积累	walk /wɔːk/ v. 走，步行	cute /kjuːt/ adj. 可爱的
	shopkeeper /ˈʃɒpkiːpə(r)/ n. 店主	bite /baɪt/ v. 咬

(　　) ① The woman wants to buy a cute little dog.

(　　) ② The shopkeeper's dog does not bite.

(　　) ③ The woman touches the dog in the shop.

(　　) ④ The dog in the shop does not bite the woman.

(　　) ⑤ The dog is the shopkeeper's.

 知识要点

　　pet作名词表示"宠物"，例如：Do you have any pets?（你有没有养宠物？）pet作动词表示"抚摸，（爱抚地）摩挲"，例如：He pets his dog.（他在摸自己的狗。）

参考译文

　　一个女人走进一家宠物店，看到一只可爱的小狗。她问店主："你的狗咬人吗？"

　　店主说："不，我的狗不咬人。"

　　女人试着摸了摸狗，狗却咬了她。

　　"哎哟！"她说，"你不是说你的狗不咬人嘛！"

　　店主说："那不是我的狗！"

答案与解析

　　❶ F　由第一段第一句可知，女人只是看到了一只可爱的小狗，并没有提出要买，本题错误。

　　❷ T　由第二段可知店主的狗不咬人，本题正确。

　　❸ T　由第三段可知，女人摸了狗，本题正确。

　　❹ F　由第三段可知，狗咬了女人，本题错误。

　　❺ F　由最后一段可知，咬女人的狗并不是店主的，本题错误。

Passage **2** 阅读短文，选择最佳答案。

　　It's eight o'clock. The children go to school by car every day. But they are walking to school today. It's ten o'clock. Mrs. Green usually stays at home in the morning. But she is going to the shops this morning. It's nine o'clock. Mr. Green usually reads his newspaper at night. But he is reading an interesting book this night.

词汇积累	usually /'juːʒuəli/ *adv.* 通常地	stay at home 在家
	newspaper /'njuːzpeɪpə(r)/ *n.* 报纸	interesting /'ɪntrəstɪŋ/ *adj.* 有趣的

(   ) ❶ How do children go to school today?

       A. They go to school by car.

       B. They go to school by bicycle.

       C. They go to school by train.

       D. They walk to school.

(   ) ❷ When do children go to school?

       A. They go to school at eight o'clock.

       B. They go to school at seven o'clock.

       C. They go to school at nine o'clock.

       D. They go to school at ten o'clock.

(   ) ❸ What does Mrs. Green do this morning?

       A. She stays at home.

       B. She goes to the shop.

       C. She reads her newspaper.

       D. She reads an interesting book.

(   ) ❹ What does Mr. Green usually do at nine o'clock at night?

       A. He reads his newspaper.

       B. He reads an interesting book.

       C. He stays at home.

       D. He goes to bed.

(   ) ⑤ What does Mr. Green do today?

             A. He goes to school.

             B. He goes to the shop.

             C. He reads his newspaper.

             D. He reads an interesting book.

 知识要点

    "by+交通运输工具"表示出行方式，例如：by bike（骑自行车），by bus（乘公共汽车），by taxi（乘出租车）。注意"步行"的表达是on foot，而不是by foot，也可以用"walk to+地点"，表示"步行去某地"，例如：I walked to the office.（我步行去办公室。）

 参考译文

    早上八点。孩子们每天都乘车去学校。但是今天他们正走着去学校。上午十点。格林太太通常上午都待在家里。但是她今早打算去商店。晚上九点。格林先生晚上通常会看报纸。但是他今晚正在看一本有趣的书。

 答案与解析

❶ D   由第三句可知选D。

❷ A   由前两句可知选A。

❸ B   由第五句和第六句可知，格林夫人上午通常待在家里，但是她今早打算去商店，B正确。

❹ A   由倒数第二句可知，格林先生经常在晚上九点看报纸，A正确。

❺ D   由最后一句可知选D。

Passage ③ 阅读短文，判断句子正（T）误（F）。

There is a young man, Lord Ye. He likes dragons very much. He draws many dragons in his house. The house becomes a world of dragons. A red dragon hears of Lord Ye and is deeply moved（感动的）. He wants to visit Lord Ye and makes a friend with him. "Hi, Mr. Ye! Nice to meet you," the real dragon comes to visit. Mr. Ye runs away as fast as he can. "Oh, my God! Help! Help!" he runs and shouts.

词汇积累		
young /jʌŋ/ *adj.* 年轻的		dragon /'dræɡən/ *n.* 龙
become /bɪ'kʌm/ *v.* 成为，变成		visit /'vɪzɪt/ *v.* 访问，拜访
run away 跑开，逃跑		shout /ʃaʊt/ *v.* 呼喊，喊叫

(   ) ❶ Lord Ye likes dinosaurs.

(   ) ❷ He draws many dragons in his school.

(   ) ❸ A green dragon wants to visit Lord Ye.

(   ) ❹ Lord Ye runs away when he sees the real dragon.

(   ) ❺ Lord Ye does not really like dragons.

 知识要点

    make a friend with（=make friends with）表示"与……交友"，例如：Can I make a friend with you?（我能和你交个朋友吗？）I want to make friends with you.（我想和你交个朋友。）

参考译文

有一个年轻人名叫叶公。他非常喜欢龙。他在家里画了许多龙。他的家变成了龙的世界。一条红色的龙听说了叶公的事，感动万分。他想拜访叶公并与他成为朋友。"嗨，叶先生！见到你很高兴，"真正的龙来拜访了。叶公飞快地逃跑了。"我的天啊！救命啊！救命啊！"他边跑边喊。

答案与解析

❶ F 由第二句可知，叶公喜欢龙，而不是喜欢恐龙，本题错误。

❷ F 由第三句可知，叶公在家里画了很多龙，而不是在学校，本题错误。

❸ F 由第五句可知，是一条红色的龙想要拜访叶公，而不是绿色的龙，本题错误。

❹ T 由倒数第二句可知本题正确。

❺ T 结合全文，叶公虽然声称自己喜欢龙，但是看到了真龙之后却跑掉了，所以他不是真的喜欢龙，本题正确。

Passage 4 阅读短文，判断句子正（T）误（F）。

Becky and Sherry are twins. Becky loves dresses. Sherry loves sports.

One day their mother said to them, "Let's buy some new clothes for you." So they went to the store together.

Their mother chose some very nice dresses for them. Becky was happy.

But Sherry was not. "How can I play baseball in this?" she asked.

Sherry looked at a boy who was trying on a pair of shorts. Sherry's mom saw this. "Well," she said, "Would you like some shorts instead?"

词汇积累	dress /dres/ *n.* 连衣裙	store /stɔː(r)/ *n.* 商店
	choose /tʃuːz/ *v.* 选择	baseball /'beɪsˌbɔːl/ *n.* 棒球
	shorts /ʃɔːts/ *n.* 短裤	instead /ɪn'sted/ *adv.* 代替

(   ) ❶ Becky and Sherry are twins.

(   ) ❷ Becky loves pants and Sherry loves dresses.

(   ) ❸ They went to the store to buy some fruits.

(   ) ❹ We can know that Sherry likes to play baseball.

(   ) ❺ Sherry bought a dress at last.

知识要点

try on表示"试穿（衣物）"，例如：Try the shoes on before you buy them.（鞋子要先穿上试一试再买。）You can try on this hat.（您可以试戴一下这顶帽子。）

 参考译文

贝姬和雪莉是双胞胎。贝姬喜欢连衣裙。雪莉喜欢运动。

一天，妈妈对她们说："我们去买些新衣服吧。"于是她们一起去了商店。

妈妈为她们挑选了一些非常漂亮的衣服。贝姬很高兴。

但是雪莉不高兴。"我穿这个怎么打棒球呢？"她问。

雪莉看着一个正在试穿短裤的男孩。雪莉的妈妈看见了，"那么，"她说，"你想要几条短裤吗？"

答案与解析

❶ T　由第一段第一句可知本题正确。

❷ F　由第一段后两句可知本题错误。

❸ F　由第二段第一句可知，她们去商店是要买新衣服，而不是买水果，本题错误。

❹ T　由第四段第二句雪莉在买新衣服的时候考虑打棒球能不能穿，可以推断她喜欢打棒球，本题正确。

❺ F　由最后一段可知，雪莉不想买裙子，因为不方便打棒球，本题错误。

Passage 5 阅读短文，选择最佳答案。

A train stops at a station. A young man wants to come out, but it is raining. A boy is standing under a big umbrella.

The young man says to the boy, "Can you go and get us two hamburgers, one for you and one for me? Here are two dollars."

"Great!" says the boy, and he goes to buy hamburgers. After some time, the boy is back. He is eating a hamburger.

"Where is my hamburger?" asks the young man.

"Oh, there is only one hamburger left. So I'm eating mine. Here is your dollar." The boy answers.

词汇 积累	station /'steɪʃn/ n. 车站	umbrella /ʌm'brelə/ n. 雨伞
	hamburger /'hæmbɜːgə(r)/ n. 汉堡包	dollar /'dɒlə(r)/ n. 美元

( ) ❶ Why does the young man want to come out of the train?

    A. Because he likes rainy days.

    B. Because he knows the boy.

    C. Because he wants to eat a hamburger.

    D. Because the train stops.

( ) ❷ What does the man want the boy to do?

    A. He wants the boy to buy hamburgers.

    B. He wants the boy to go away.

    C. He wants to give the boy two dollars.

    D. All the above are right.

(   ) ③ Why does the man give the boy two dollars?

        A. Because he wants the boy to buy an umbrella.

        B. Because he wants the boy to buy two hamburgers, so he can eat one.

        C. Because one hamburger is two dollars.

        D. Because the boy asks the man for two dollars.

(   ) ④ How much is one hamburger?

        A. Three dollars.   B. Two dollars.

        C. Five dollars.   D. One dollar.

(   ) ⑤ What do you know from this story?

        A. The man gets what he wants.

        B. The man is happy.

        C. The boy is silly.

        D. The man does not eat a hamburger.

 知识要点

    station和stop都指"车站"，两者的区别是：station通常指火车站或汽车站，例如：Mom met me at the station.（妈妈在车站接了我。）而stop通常指公共汽车站，尤指中途停车站，例如：They waited at a bus stop.（他们在一个公共汽车站等车。）

 参考译文

    火车靠站了。一个年轻人想出站，但是正在下雨。一个男孩撑着一把大伞站在雨里。

    这个年轻人对男孩说："你能去给我们两个买两个汉堡吗？一个给你，一个给我。这里是两美元。"

　　"太好了！"男孩说，接着他就去买汉堡了。过了一会儿，男孩回来了，他正在吃汉堡。

　　"我的汉堡在哪儿呢？"年轻人问道。

　　"哦，只剩下一个汉堡了。所以我吃的是我的汉堡。给你剩下的一美元。"男孩回答道。

 答案与解析

　　❶ C　由第一段可知，年轻人并不认识男孩，排除B；火车停靠与年轻人想出站并没有直接关系，排除D。A在文中并未提及。由第二段可知，年轻人出站是想吃汉堡，C正确。

　　❷ A　由第二段可知选A。

　　❸ B　由第二段可知选B。文中并未提及年轻人想让男孩买雨伞，排除A。年轻人让男孩买两个汉堡，给了男孩两美元，可以推断一个汉堡一美元，排除C。男孩并没有向年轻人要钱，排除D。

　　❹ D　通过对第三题选项C的分析，可知一个汉堡一美元，D正确。

　　❺ D　结合全文，年轻人并没有得到自己想要的汉堡，也不开心，排除A和B。男孩是否愚蠢在文中并未提及，排除C。年轻人没有吃到汉堡，D正确。

 **Passage 6** 阅读短文，选择最佳答案。

When Grandma Was a Girl

Jay and Susie opened the door. It was Grandma! They asked her to tell a story. She told them a story about her life. It took place many years ago.

Grandma was a little girl. She lived on a farm. She had three brothers. All of them had chores to do. Grandma fed the chickens and collected their eggs.

One day, Grandma found a rock in one chicken's nest. She was confused. How did that get there?

Then her brothers told her it was a joke. Grandma laughed. When they heard the story, Jay and Susie laughed too.

词汇积累		
take place 发生		chore /tʃɔː(r)/ n. 家务活；杂事
feed /fiːd/ 喂养		collect /kəˈlekt/ v. 收集
rock /rɒk/ n. 岩石		confused /kənˈfjuzd/ adj. 困惑的
joke /dʒəʊk/ n. 玩笑		laugh /lɑːf/ v. 大笑

( ) ❶ Grandma told Jay and Susie a story about _____.

    A. her school life   B. Christmas

    C. her life   D. a picnic

( ) ❷ Grandma has _____.

    A. two brothers and a sister   B. three sisters

    C. two sisters and a brother   D. three brothers

(   ) ③ Grandma had to _____.

       A. catch the chickens   B. feed the chickens

       C. walk the dog   D. clean the yard

(   ) ④ One day, grandma found a/an _____ in one chicken's nest.

       A. cat   B. egg

       C. rock   D. rooster（公鸡）

(   ) ⑤ Which of the following is true?

       A. Grandma's father put the rock in the nest.

       B. Grandma's brothers were confused about the rock.

       C. Grandma gave the rock to her mother.

       D. Jay and Susie laughed at the story.

 知识要点

     take place和happen都表示"发生"，happen更倾向于偶然发生的、不确定的事情。例如：When did this event take place?（这件事是什么时候发生的？）An earthquake happened last night.（昨晚发生了地震。）

参考译文

当奶奶还是个小女孩

     杰伊和苏茜打开了门。是奶奶！他们让她讲个故事。她给他们讲了她生活中的故事。那是很多年前的事了。

     奶奶那时是个小女孩。她住在一个农场里。她有三个兄弟。他们都有家务要做。奶奶喂鸡，捡鸡蛋。

     有一天，奶奶在一个鸡窝里发现了一块石头。她很困惑。石头怎么会在这里？

     然后她的兄弟们告诉她这是个玩笑。奶奶笑了。当听到这个故事时，杰伊和苏茜也笑了。

Part 1 主题阅读

答案与解析

❶ C 由第一段第四句可知，奶奶告诉他们的是关于自己生活的故事，C正确。

❷ D 由第二段第三句可知选D。

❸ B 由第二段最后一句可知选B。

❹ C 由第三段第一句可知选C。

❺ D 由最后一段最后一句可知选D。由第四段第一句可知，是奶奶兄弟们放的石头，A错误；由第三段第二句可知，鸡窝里出现了石头，奶奶很困惑，B错误；C项文中并未提及。

 Passage 7 阅读短文，选择最佳答案。

My uncle lives in a village, but he works in a big city. He goes to work by train every morning and comes home in the same way.

One morning, my uncle is reading a newspaper on the train. A man behind him says "hello" to him and begins to talk to him. "Your life isn't interesting, is it? You take the same train every morning, and you always sit in the same seat and read the same paper."

"How do you know all that?" My uncle asks.

"Because I always sit in the same seat behind you," the man says.

词汇积累	village /'vɪlɪdʒ/ n. 村庄 begin /bɪ'gɪn/ v. 开始	in the same way 用同样的方式 always /'ɔːlweɪz/ adv. 一直，总是

(　　) ❶ How does my uncle come home?

　　A. He comes home by car.　　　　B. He comes home by train.

　　C. He comes home by plane.　　　D. He comes home by bicycle.

(　　) ❷ What does my uncle usually do on the train?

　　A. He talks to the man.　　　　B. He reads a newspaper.

　　C. He sleeps.　　　　　　　　D. He works.

(　　) ❸ Why does the man think my uncle's life isn't interesting?

　　A. Because my uncle takes the same train.

　　B. Because my uncle sits in the same seat.

　　C. Because my uncle reads the same paper.

　　D. All the above are right.

(　　) ❹ What can you know about this man?

　　A. He sits in the same seat every day.

　　B. He does not like my uncle.

　　C. He works in a big city.

　　D. He reads the newspaper, too.

(　　) ❺ What do you know from this story?

　　A. This man's life isn't interesting, either.

　　B. Do not talk to others on the train.

　　C. Go to work by train isn't interesting.

　　D. We should not read a newspaper.

知识要点

表示乘坐交通工具时，"on+交通工具"通常指可以在其中走动，例如：on the bus（在公共汽车上），on the plane（在飞机上），on the train（在火车上）。"in+交通工具"通常指不可以在其中走动，例如：in the car（在汽车里）。

 参考译文

　　我叔叔住在一个小乡村，但他在一个大城市工作。每天早上他都乘坐火车上班，同样坐火车回家。

　　一天早上，我叔叔正在火车上看报纸。坐在他后面的人跟他打招呼，并开始跟他交谈。"你的生活很没意思，是不是？你每天早上都乘坐同样的火车，总是坐在相同的位置上，还读着同样的报纸。"

　　"你怎么知道这些的？"我叔叔问。

　　"因为我也总是坐在一个位置上，就在你后面。"这个人回答。

答案与解析

❶ B　由第一段第二句可知选B，"in the same way"是答题线索。

❷ B　由第二段最后一句可知选B。

❸ D　由第二段最后一句可知，A、B、C都正确，本题选D。

❹ A　由最后一段可知选A。B、C、D文中并未提及。

❺ A　本题属于推理题，这个男人认为叔叔每天坐同一班火车的同一个位置读同样的报纸，他觉得叔叔的人生很无趣，那他同样一直坐在叔叔后面的位置，他的人生也同样无趣。

Passage 阅读短文，回答问题。

Amy is not happy. She cannot find her favourite pen. She looks all over the house. She looks under the bed. She looks in her desk. She looks in the kitchen and in her book bag. But she cannot find it. Amy is really upset. Amy wants to cry. She cries to her mother, "Mom, my pen is lost." Mom says, "Don't cry. I will help you look for it." When Mom goes downstairs, she laughs. "Why are you laughing, Mom?" Mom says, "Check behind your ear." And as Amy checks her ear, she finds her pen. She had put it there earlier.

Now she is happy.

词汇 积累	upset /ˌʌp'set/ *adj.* 沮丧的	lost /lɒst/ *adj.* 丢失的
	laughs /lɑːf/ *v.* 笑	check /tʃek/ *v.* 检查

1 Why is Amy not happy?

_____

2 Is the pen in the desk?

_____

3 Who helps Amy find her pen?

_____

4 Where is the pen?

_____

5 How does Amy feel when she finds her pen?

_____

Part 1 主题阅读

 知识要点

look for表示"寻找"，强调找的动作和过程，例如：She looks for her glasses.（她找她的眼镜。）find表示"找到；发现"，强调找的结果，例如：Finally, she found a good job after one year.（最终，在一年后，她找到了一份好工作。）

 参考译文

埃米不高兴，因为她找不到她最喜欢的笔了。她把房子每个角落都找了。床底下、书桌里、厨房里和书包里，全都找了，但她找不到。埃米真的很难过，很想哭。她哭着对妈妈说："妈妈，我的笔丢了。"妈妈说，"别哭，我会帮你找的。"妈妈下楼的时候笑了。"妈妈，你为什么笑？"妈妈说，"看看你耳朵后面有什么。"当埃米摸她的耳朵时，她找到了她的笔。她之前把它放在那儿的。

现在她高兴了。

答案与解析

❶ Because she cannot find her favourite pen.　由第一段前两句可知答案。

❷ No, it isn't.　由第一段第五句至第七句可知本题为否定回答。

❸ Her mom./Her mother.　结合全文可知答案。

❹ It's behind Amy's ear.　由第一段倒数第二句和第三句可知答案。

❺ She is happy.　由最后一段可知答案。

It is Sunday. There are many people on the bus. An old man is looking here and there. He wants to find an empty seat. Then he finds one. He goes to it. A small bag is on the seat. And a young man is beside it.

"Is this seat empty?" asks the old man.

"No, it's for an old woman. She went to buy some bananas," says the man.

"Well, let me sit here, please. I'll leave here when she comes back." says the old man.

The bus starts. "She has not come, but her bag is here. Let me give her the bag." Then the old man throws the bag out.

The young man shouts, "Don't throw it! It is my bag!"

词汇积累	empty /'empti/ *adj.* 空的	leave /liːv/ *v.* 离开
	start /stɑːt/ *v.* 开始	throw /θrəʊ/ *v.* 投；掷；抛；扔

( ) ❶ The old man does not find an empty seat.

( ) ❷ There is a young man beside the small bag.

( ) ❸ The old man does not want to leave the seat.

( ) ❹ The small bag belongs to（属于）the young man.

( ) ❺ There is not an old woman.

知识要点

here and there表示"各处，到处"，例如：The children are jumping here and there.（孩子们到处跳。）He often runs here and there.（他经常到处跑。）

参考译文

星期天，公共汽车上有很多人。一位老人正在环顾四周。他想找到一个空位，随后就找到了一个。他走了过去。座位上有一个小包。一个年轻人坐在旁边。

"这个座位有人吗？"老人问。

"不，这是给一个老妇人留的。她去买一些香蕉。"年轻人回答。

"好吧，请先让我坐在这里，等她回来时我会离开。"老人说。

公共汽车开动了。"她还没有来，但是她的包在这里。我把包给她。"然后老人把包扔了出去。

年轻人喊道："别扔！这是我的包！"

答案与解析

① F　由第一段第五句可知，老人找到了空座位，本题错误。

② T　由第一段最后两句可知本题正确。

③ F　由第四段可知，老人提议自己先坐一会儿，等老妇人回来他就会离开，所以老人没有不愿意离开座位，本题错误。

④ T　由最后一段可知本题正确。

⑤ T　结合全文，小包是年轻人的，所以年轻人在撒谎，根本没有老妇人，本题正确。

Passage 10 阅读短文，选择最佳答案。

Mr. White is very rich. One day, the Whites move to a new town. Beth, his daughter, is also going to a new school in the town. On the first day, Mr. White says to Beth, "Beth, don't say we are rich. You must be modest. You must be kind to others." Beth says, "I see, Dad."

Then Beth goes to school. Her teacher introduces her to other classmates, "This is Beth. She's our new classmate." The classmates clap their hands, "Welcome to our class!" Beth says happily, "Thank you. I have just moved to the town with my parents. My family is very poor. My father is very poor. My mother is very poor. The gardener is very poor. The cook is poor and all the other servants are poor, too."

词汇 积累	rich /rɪtʃ/ *adj.* 富裕的	modest /'mɒdɪst/ *adj.* 谦虚的
	introduce /ˌɪntrə'djuːs/ *v.* 介绍	poor /pɔː(r)/ *adj.* 贫穷的
	gardener /'gɑːdnə(r)/ *n.* 园丁	servant /'sɜːvənt/ *n.* 仆人

( )❶ What do you know about Mr. White?

    A. He is very poor.

    B. He does not move to a new town.

    C. He has a daughter.

    D. His daughter's name is Amy.

( ) ② What does Mr. White want Beth to do?

A. He wants Beth to be modest.

B. He wants Beth to say they are rich.

C. He wants Beth to be bad to others.

D. He wants Beth not to say anything to others.

( ) ③ How does Beth feel when she introduces herself?

A. She is shy.   B. She is happy.

C. She is angry.   D. She is sad.

( ) ④ How many people in Beth's family?

A. There are four people in Beth's family.

B. There are five people in Beth's family.

C. There are six people in Beth's family.

D. We do not know.

( ) ⑤ How will Beth's classmates think about her?

A. Beth is very poor.   B. Beth is very rich.

C. They like Beth.   D. They do not like Beth.

 知识要点

"the+姓氏复数"表示"某姓氏一家人"。例如：The Smiths came to see me yesterday.（史密斯一家人昨天来看我。）The Greens are having dinner.（格林一家正在吃晚饭。）

 参考译文

怀特先生非常有钱。一天，怀特一家搬到了一个新城镇。他的女儿贝丝也要到城里的新学校读书。上学第一天，怀特先生对贝丝说："贝丝，不要说我们很富有。你必须谦逊。你必须友善待人。"贝丝说："我明白了，爸爸。"

于是贝丝去上学了。她的老师将她介绍给其他的同学："这是贝丝，她是我们的新同学。"同学们鼓掌欢迎："欢迎你到我们班上来！"贝丝愉快地说："谢谢你们。我刚和父母搬到这个城镇。我家很穷，我的爸爸很穷，我的妈妈很穷，我家的园丁很穷，厨师很穷，其他的佣人们也很穷。"

 答案与解析

❶ C 由第一段前三句可知，与文章内容匹配的是C。

❷ A 由第一段倒数第二句怀特先生说的话可知选A。B、C与文意相反，D不符合文意。

❸ B 由第二段中间部分 "Beth says happily..." 可知选B。

❹ D 由第二段后半部分贝丝说的话可知，她家里有爸爸、妈妈、园丁、厨师，还有其他佣人，总人数在文中并未提及，D正确。

❺ B 通过对第四题的分析可知，同学们会认为贝丝家里很富有，B正确。A与文意相反，C、D文中并未提及。

Passage 11 阅读短文，判断句子正（T）误（F）。

An old man is selling a big cow. A young man comes to the cow and begins to look at it carefully. Then the old man goes up to him and says in his ears. "Don't say anything about the cow before I sell it, then I will give you some meat."

"All right," says the young man. After the old man sells the cow, he gives the young man some meat and says, "Now, you can tell me how you think of the bad leg of the cow."

"I didn't find the bad leg," says the young man.

"Then why did you look at the cow carefully?" asks the old man.

Then young man answers, "Because I have never seen a cow, and I wanted to know what it looked like."

词汇 积累		
sell /sel/ v. 出售，售卖		cow /kaʊ/ n. 奶牛
carefully /'keəfəli/ adv. 仔细地		answer /'ɑːnsə(r)/ v. 回答

(　　) ❶ The old man wants the young man to say something about the cow.

(　　) ❷ The old man does not give the young man some meat.

(　　) ❸ The young man does what the old man tells him to do.

(　　) ❹ The young man finds the bad leg of the cow.

(　　) ❺ The young man wants to buy this cow.

知识要点

begin to do sth.表示"开始做某事"，例如：He must now begin to get ready.（他现在就必须开始准备。）I began to learn English last week. （我上周开始学英语。）

参考译文

一位老人正在卖一头大奶牛。一个年轻人来到奶牛旁边开始仔细地看它。然后老人走过去对他耳语道："在我卖掉这头奶牛前不要说任何话，过后我会给你一些肉。"

"好吧。"年轻男子说道。老人卖掉了奶牛，他给了年轻人一些肉并说道："现在你可以跟我说说你是怎么看待这头奶牛的坏腿的。"

"我没发现坏腿呀。"年轻男子说。

"那你为什么仔细地看着这头牛？"老人问道。

年轻人回答道："因为我从未见过奶牛，我想知道它长什么样。"

答案与解析

❶ F　由第一段最后一句可知，老人让年轻人在自己卖出奶牛之前什么都不要说，本题错误。

❷ F　由第二段第二句可知，老人在卖掉奶牛之后给了年轻人一些肉，本题错误。

❸ T　结合全文，年轻人做了老人让他做的事情，本题正确。

❹ F　由第三段年轻人说的话可知，他并没有发现牛的坏腿，本题错误。

❺ F　由最后一段年轻人说的话可知，他是想知道奶牛长什么样子，而不是想买牛，本题错误。

Unit 09　轻松故事

One day, a monkey rides his bike near the river. He sees a lion under a tree. The lion runs at him. He is afraid and falls into the river. He can't swim. He shouts. The rabbit hears him. He jumps into the river and swims to the monkey. But the rabbit can't help him. Luckily, an elephant comes along. He is very strong. He helps the rabbit and monkey. Three friends are very happy. They go to the elephant's home. Then, three of them become good friends.

词汇积累	ride /raɪd/ v. 骑（自行车、摩托车或马）	afraid /əˈfreɪd/ adj. 害怕的
	jump /dʒʌmp/ v. 跳	luckily /ˈlʌkɪli/ adv. 幸运地

❶ Where is the lion?

_____

❷ Why does the monkey fall into the river?

_____

❸ Why cannot the rabbit help the monkey?

_____

❹ What does the elephant do?

_____

5 Where do the three of them go?

_____

知识要点

come along在文中表示"出现"，例如：Here comes along a mouse.（这里出现了一只老鼠。）come along还表示"跟随"，例如：I'm glad you came along.（有你跟我一起来，我很高兴。）

参考译文

一天，一只猴子在河边骑自行车。他看到树下有只狮子。狮子朝他跑来。他很害怕，掉进了河里。他不会游泳，于是大声喊叫。兔子听到他的声音，跳进河里，游向猴子。但是兔子救不了他。幸运的是，大象来了。他很强壮。他救出了兔子和猴子。三个朋友很高兴。他们去了大象家做客。然后，他们三个成为好朋友。

答案与解析

1 The lion is under a tree.　由第二句可知答案。

2 Because he is afraid./Because he is afraid of the lion.　由第四句可知答案。

3 Because the rabbit is not strong.　本题为推理题，由后文可知大象很强壮，救了猴子和兔子，所以兔子救不了猴子是因为他不强壮。

4 He helps the rabbit and the monkey.　由倒数第四句可知答案。

5 They go to the elephant's home.　由倒数第二句可知答案。

Passage 2　阅读短文，回答问题。

A little panda picks up a pumpkin and wants to take it home. But the pumpkin is too big. The panda cannot take it home. Suddenly she sees a bear riding a bike toward her. She watches the bike. "I know! I have a good idea." she jumps and shouts happily, "I can roll a pumpkin. It's like a wheel."

So she rolls the pumpkin to her home. When her mother sees the big pumpkin, she is surprised, "Oh, my God! How can you carry it home?" The little panda answers, "I cannot lift it, but I can roll it." Her mother smiles and says, "What a clever girl!"

> **词汇 积累**
> roll /rəʊl/ v. （使）翻滚，滚动　　　　wheel /wiːl/ n. 轮，轮子
> carry /ˈkæri/ v. 拿；扛　　　　　　　　lift /lɪft/ v. 提起，举起

① What does the panda pick up?

_____

② Why cannot the panda take the pumpkin home?

_____

③ What's the panda's good idea?

_____

④ Where does the panda go?

_____

⑤ How does the panda's mother feel?

_____

知识要点

　　roll在文中作动词，表示"（使）翻滚，（使）滚动"，例如：The ball rolled down the hill.（球滚下了山。）roll还可以作名词，表示"翻滚，打滚；卷，卷轴"，例如：The kittens are enjoying a roll in the sunshine.（那些小猫在阳光下嬉戏打滚。）Please buy a roll of film for me.（请给我买一卷胶卷。）

参考译文

　　一只小熊猫摘了一个大南瓜，想把它拿回家。但是这个南瓜太大了，小熊猫没有办法把这么大的南瓜带回家。突然她看见一只熊骑着一辆自行车朝她这边来。她看着自行车，跳了起来，开心地说："有了！我有办法了。我可以把南瓜滚回家去。南瓜就像车轮一样。"

　　于是她把南瓜滚回了家。她妈妈看到这个大南瓜，非常惊讶："天啊！你是怎么把它带回家的？"小熊猫回答："我拎不动它，可是我能滚动它啊！"她妈妈微笑着说："真是个聪明的小姑娘！"

答案与解析

① She picks up a pumpkin.　由第一段第一句可知答案。

② Because the pumpkin is too big.　由第一段第二句和第三句可知答案。

③ She rolls the pumpkin.　由第一段最后一句可知答案。

④ She goes home.　由第二段第一句可知答案。

⑤ She feels happy.　由第二段最后一句可知，熊猫的妈妈为自己的女儿感到开心。本题大意正确即可。

Passage 3 阅读短文，回答问题。

A little frog wakes up in the morning. He cannot find his toy and is crying. A fish hears and comes. He asks, "Why are you crying?"

The frog answers, "I lost my toy."

"What is your toy?"

"I don't know its name, but it is round and yellow."

The fish says, "I know, I know." He comes back with a yellow leaf.

"No, no. That's not my toy." The frog still cries.

A dog is coming, "The round and yellow thing is on the playground. That must be your toy."

The frog sees it, but that is not his toy, too. It is a yellow ball.

A squirrel is running with a pine nut. But that's not the frog's toy.

It is dark. The frog is very sad. He does not find his toy. He cries again. The moon is rising in the sky. The shadow of the moon is on the pond. "Oh! My toy! I found my toy!" The frog jumps happily.

词汇 积累	lose /luːz/ v. 遗失，丢失	round /raʊnd/ adj. 圆形的
	still /stɪl/ adv. 仍然	squirrel /ˈskwɪrəl/ n. 松鼠
	pine nut 松子，松仁	shadow /ˈʃædəʊ/ n. 阴影，影子

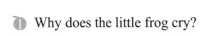

① Why does the little frog cry?

_____

② What does the frog's toy look like?

_____

③ What is on the playground?

_____

④ What is the squirrel doing?

_____

⑤ What is the little frog's toy?

_____

 知识要点

　　情态动词must表示"必须"，后面跟动词原形，语气非常强烈，例如：You must go home today.（你今天一定要回家。）must还表示"可能，想必"，是一种合理、有根据的推测，例如：Susan plays tennis every day. She must like to play tennis.（苏珊每天打网球，她一定很喜欢打网球。）

 参考译文

　　一只小青蛙早上醒来之后，找不到自己的玩具，于是开始哭泣。一条鱼听到他的哭声后赶来。他问道："你为什么哭？"

　　青蛙回答："我弄丢了我的玩具。"

　　"你的玩具是什么？"

　　"我不知道它的名字，但它圆圆的，黄黄的。"

　　鱼说："我知道了，我知道了。"他带回了一片黄色的叶子。

　　"不，不，那不是我的玩具。"青蛙继续哭。

　　一条狗来了，"操场上有一个圆圆的、黄黄的东西。那一定是你的玩具。"

青蛙看了后，发现那也不是他的玩具。这是一个黄色的球。

一只松鼠带着松子奔跑。但这不是青蛙的玩具。

天黑了。青蛙很伤心。他没有找到玩具。他又开始哭了。月亮在天空中升起。月亮的影子落在了池塘上。"哦！我的玩具！我找到了我的玩具！"青蛙高兴地跳了起来。

 答案与解析

① Because he loses his toy.　由第一段第二句和第二段可知答案。

② It is round and yellow.　由第四段可知答案。

③ It is a yellow ball./A yellow ball.　由倒数第三段可知答案。

④ It is running with a pine nut.　由倒数第二段第一句可知答案。

⑤ The shadow of the moon is the little frog's toy./The shadow of the moon.
由最后一段可知答案。

Passage 阅读短文，选择最佳答案。

Sam is a little fish. He lives in the sea. He is very lonely and wants to have a friend. The friend should look like him. Sam sees an ink fish. The ink fish has eight legs. He does not look like Sam. So Sam swims away.

Sam meets a shark. He wants to say hello to the shark. The shark opens his big mouth and wants to eat Sam. Sam runs away quickly.

Sam is tired and hungry. He wants to have a rest. Then he sees a round fish. She says to him, "Hello! Would you like to be my friend?"

Sam answers, "Of course! But you are round. I am flat."

The round fish says, "But we are both fishes."

Sam thinks and says, "You are right. Let us be friends." They become good friends.

词汇积累		
lonely /ˈləʊnli/ *adj.* 孤独的		ink fish 墨鱼
quickly /ˈkwɪkli/ *adv.* 迅速地		flat /flæt/ *adj.* 扁平的

(   ) ❶ Why does Sam want a friend?

      A. Because he is a little fish.

      B. Because he is very lonely.

      C. Because he is tired and hungry.

      D. Because he wants to have a rest.

( ) ❷ Why does't Sam want to be friends with ink fish?

A. Because ink fish does not look like him.

B. Because ink fish is ugly.

C. Because ink fish opens his big mouth.

D. Because ink fish is round.

( ) ❸ Why does the shark open his mouth?

A. Because he wants to be friends with Sam.

B. Because he wants Sam to see his teeth.

C. Because he wants to eat Sam.

D. Because he wants to drink water.

( ) ❹ What happens between Sam and the round fish?

A. Sam runs away from the round fish.

B. They do not become friends.

C. The round fish shows her eight legs to Sam.

D. They become friends.

( ) ❺ What do you know from this story?

A. Friends can be different.

B. We cannot be friends with ink fish.

C. The ink fish is shark's friend.

D. The round fish does not like Sam.

知识要点

say hello to sb. 表示"和某人打招呼，向某人问好"，例如：Please say hello to everybody.（请向大家问好。）Pupils say hello to their teacher.（学生们向老师问好。）

 参考译文

　　萨姆是一条小鱼。他住在海里。他很寂寞，想要一个朋友。他的朋友应该长得像他。萨姆看见一条墨鱼。墨鱼有八条腿。墨鱼和萨姆一点也不像。于是萨姆游走了。

　　萨姆遇到一条鲨鱼。他想和鲨鱼打招呼。鲨鱼却张大嘴巴，想吃萨姆。萨姆马上逃开了。

　　萨姆又累又饿。他想休息一下。然后他看到一条圆形的鱼。她对他说："你好！你想和我做朋友吗？"

　　萨姆回答："当然！但是你是圆的。我是扁的。"

　　圆形鱼说："但是我们都是鱼呀。"

　　萨姆想了想，说："你说得对。让我们成为朋友吧。"于是他们就成为好朋友。

 答案与解析

❶ B　由第一段第三句可知选B。

❷ A　由第一段可知，萨姆想找个跟自己很像的朋友，墨鱼和自己不像，所以萨姆不和他当朋友，A正确。B文中并未提及。由第二段可知，是鲨鱼张开了自己的大嘴，不是墨鱼，C错误。墨鱼不是圆形的，D错误。

❸ C　由第二段第三句可知选C。

❹ D　由最后一段可知，萨姆最后和圆形鱼成了朋友，B错误，D正确。由第二段可知，萨姆是从鲨鱼身边游走了，A错误。由第一段可知，墨鱼有八条腿，不是圆形鱼有八条腿，C错误。

❺ A　本文主要讲述了虽然萨姆和圆形鱼长得不一样，但是他们最后也能做朋友，即我们要接受别人的不同，朋友可以与我们不一样，A符合大意。B、C文中并未提及。圆形鱼愿意和萨姆做朋友，她不讨厌萨姆，D错误。

Passage 5 阅读短文，回答问题。

One day, Dora's mother gives her a coin. It is a bit dirty, so Dora washes it. Then it starts talking to Dora.

Today I talk to a coin. When it is made, it is nice and clean. People take the coin to a bank. It stays there for a few days. Then the bank gives the coin to a man. My mother goes to buy some cake from the man's shop. The man gives the coin to her as part of her change. She drops the coin. A street cleaner sees it and picks it up. He returns it to my mother. She gives it to me as pocket money. I wash the coin to make it clean again.

词汇积累	coin /kɔɪn/ n. 硬币	dirty /'dɜːti/ adj. 脏的
	wash /wɒʃ/ v. 洗	bank /bæŋk/ n. 银行
	change /tʃeɪndʒ/ n. 零钱	street cleaner 街头清洁工
	return /rɪ'tɜːn/ v. 退还	pocket money 零花钱

1 Why does Dora wash the coin?

_____

2 Who does the bank give the coin to?

_____

3 What does Dora's mother want to buy?

_____

4 Why does the man give Dora's mother this coin?

_____

 Why does Dora's mother give this coin to her?

知识要点

  change在文中作名词，表示"找给的零钱"，例如：Don't forget to count your change.（别忘了数一数你的零钱。）change作名词还表示"变化"，例如：The same changes took place again and again .（同样的变化一再发生。）

 参考译文

  一天，多拉的妈妈给了她一枚硬币。它有点脏，所以多拉洗了洗它。然后，硬币开始与多拉聊天。

  今天我和一枚硬币聊天了。它刚被锻造出来的时候，既漂亮又干净。人们将硬币送到银行。它在那里待了几天。然后，银行将硬币交给一个男人。我妈妈去那人的商店买了些蛋糕。这个男人将硬币作为零钱找给了她。她掉了硬币。街头清洁工看到并捡起了它。他把它还给了我妈妈。妈妈把硬币当作零用钱给了我。我把硬币再次洗干净了。

 答案与解析

  ❶ Because it is a bit dirty. 由第一段第二句可知答案。

  ❷ The bank gives the coin to a man. 由第二段第五句可知答案。

  ❸ She wants to buy some cake. 由第二段第六句可知答案。

  ❹ He gives the coin to Dora's mother as part of her change. 由第二段倒数第七句可知答案。

  ❺ She gives it to Dora as pocket money. 由第二段倒数第二句可知答案。

Unit 10   哲理故事

 Passage ①   阅读短文，回答问题。

Thirsty Crow

The crow feels very thirsty. He looks for water everywhere. Finally, he finds a pitcher. But there is not a lot of water in the pitcher. His beak could not reach it. He tries again and again, but still could not touch the water. When he is about to give up, an idea comes to him. He takes a pebble and drops it into the pitcher. Then he takes another and drops it in. The water rises, and the crow can drink the water.

词汇 积累	thirsty /'θɜːsti/ *adj.* 口渴的	finally /'faɪnəli/ *adv.* 最终
	pitcher /'pɪtʃə(r)/ *n.* 罐	beak /biːk/ *n.* 鸟喙
	reach /riːtʃ/ *v.* 够得到	pebble /'pebl/ *n.* 鹅卵石

① Why does the crow look for water?

_____

② Why couldn't the crow reach the water?

_____

③ What does the crow take?

_____

④ Why does the water rise?

_____

⑤ Is the crow thirsty at the end of the story?

_____

 知识要点

be about to do sth.表示"将要做某事",由于本身已经含有"即将"这样的时间概念,通常不与表示具体时间的状语连用。例如:He's about to go.(他就要走了。)We are about to start.(我们即将动身。)

 **参考译文**

口渴的乌鸦

一只乌鸦非常口渴,到处找水喝。终于,他找到了一个大水罐。然而,水罐里面的水并不多,他的嘴够不到水面,他试了一次又一次,都没有成功。就在他想放弃的时候,他突然想到一个主意。乌鸦叼来了一块石子投到水罐里,接着又叼了一块石子放进去。水面升高了,乌鸦喝到了水。

 答案与解析

❶ Because he feels very thirsty.　第一句第二句互为因果。

❷ Because there is not a lot of water in the pitcher.　第四句和第五句互为因果。

❸ A pebble.　由倒数第三句可知答案。

❹ Because the crow drops two pebbles in the pitcher.　本题要对倒数第二句和第三句进行总结,大意正确即可。

❺ No, he isn't.　由最后一句可知,乌鸦喝到了水,所以他不再口渴了。

 **Passage 2** 阅读短文，回答问题。

One hot summer day, a fox is walking through an orchard（果园）. He stops before a bunch of grapes. They are ripe and juicy.

"I'm feeling thirsty," he thinks. So he backs up a few paces, gets a running start, jumps up, but cannot reach the grapes.

He walks back. One, two, three, he jumps up again, but still, he misses the grapes. The fox tries again and again, but never succeeds. At last, he gives it up.

He walks away and says, "I am sure they are sour."

词汇积累		
ripe /raɪp/ *adj.* 成熟的	juicy /ˈdʒuːsi/ *adj.* 多汁的
pace /peɪs/	miss /mɪs/
n.（走或跑时）迈出的一步	*v.* 未击中；未得到
succeed /səkˈsiːd/ *v.* 办到，做成	sour /ˈsaʊə(r)/ *adj.* 酸的

❶ Why does the fox stop before a bunch of grapes?

_____

❷ Are the grapes delicious?

_____

❸ What does the fox do to get the grapes?

_____

❹ Why does the fox give up?

_____

⑤ Why does the fox say the grapes are sour?

_____

 知识要点

give up表示"放弃"，例如：I give up—tell me the answer.（我放弃了，把答案告诉我吧。）She doesn't give up easily.（她不轻易认输。）

 参考译文

炎热夏日的一天，一只狐狸正穿过果园。他停在一串葡萄前。葡萄成熟了，汁水丰富。

他想："我有些口渴。"于是他后退了几步，蓄力奔跑，跳跃，却够不到葡萄。

他走回去。一、二、三，他又跳了起来，仍然够不到葡萄。狐狸一次又一次地尝试，一直没成功。最后，他放弃了。

他走开了，并说："这些葡萄肯定是酸的。"

 答案与解析

① Because he is thirsty and wants to eat the grapes. 本题需要对前两段进行总结，大意正确即可。

② Yes, they are. 由第一段最后一句可知，葡萄成熟了且汁水丰富，本题为肯定回答。

③ He backs up a few paces, gets a running start, and jumps up. 由第二段最后一句可知答案。

④ Because he never succeeds. 由第三段倒数第二句可知答案。

⑤ Because he cannot get the grapes. 结合全文可以总结出答案，本题大意正确即可。

Passage 3 阅读短文，判断句子正（T）误（F）。

A man has two dogs: a hound and a housedog. He trains the hound to help him hunt and teaches the housedog to watch the house. When he returns home after a day's hunt, he always gives the housedog some meat. The hound feels very angry. He says unhappily to the housedog, "When I work very hard outside, you share my food." "Don't blame（责备）me, my friend. You should blame the master. He doesn't teach me to hunt, but to share other's food," the housedog answers.

词汇积累	hound /haʊnd/ *n.* 猎犬，猎狗	train /treɪn/ *v.* 训练
	hunt /hʌnt/ *v.* 打猎	master /ˈmɑːstə(r)/ *n.* 主人

(   ) ❶ The hound helps the man watch the house.

(   ) ❷ The man gives the housedog some meat after returning home.

(   ) ❸ The hound is happy when the housedog has meat.

(   ) ❹ The hound should not blame the housedog.

(   ) ❺ The housedog does nothing at all.

 知识要点

train在文中作动词，表示"训练"，例如：She trains horses.（她是驯马的。）train作名词表示"火车；列车"，例如：I like travelling by train.（我喜欢乘火车旅行。）

 参考译文

　　一个人养了两只狗：一只猎犬和一只家犬。他训练猎犬来帮助他狩猎，并教家犬看家。在一天的狩猎之后，这个人回到家总是会给家犬分一些肉。猎犬感到非常生气。他很不高兴地对家犬说："我在外面辛苦工作，你却分享我的食物。""别怪我，我的朋友。你应该责怪主人。他没教我打猎，只教了怎么分享别人的食物。"家犬答道。

 答案与解析

　　❶ F　由第二句可知，这个人训练猎犬打猎，家犬看家，而不是训练猎犬看家，本题错误。

　　❷ T　由第三句可知本题正确。

　　❸ F　由第四句中的"angry"和第五句中的"unhappily"可知，猎犬非常生气，他很不开心，本题错误。

　　❹ T　由最后家犬说的话可知本题正确。

　　❺ F　由第二句可知，家犬会看家，并不是什么都没做，本题错误。

Part 1 主题阅读

Passage 4 阅读短文，判断句子正（T）误（F）。

A bird is in a cage outside a window. She often sings at night when all other birds are asleep. One night a bat comes. He asks the bird why she is silent by day and sings only at night.

The bird answers, "Last year when I was singing in the daytime, a bird catcher heard my voice and caught me in his net. Since then, I have never sung by day."

The bat says, "But it is useless to do this now that you have become a prisoner." Then he flies away.

词汇积累		
cage /keɪdʒ/ *n.* 笼子		asleep /əˈsliːp/ *adj.* 睡着的
bat /bæt/ *n.* 蝙蝠		silent /ˈsaɪlənt/ *adj.* 沉默的
daytime /ˈdeɪtaɪm/ *n.* 白天		voice /vɔɪs/ *n.* 声音
useless /ˈjuːsləs/ *adj.* 无用的		prisoner /ˈprɪznə(r)/ *n.* 囚犯，犯人

(　　) ❶ The bird lives in a cage.

(　　) ❷ The bird sings in the morning.

(　　) ❸ The bird catcher got the bird.

(　　) ❹ The bat thinks the bird is right.

(　　) ❺ The bird cannot fly away.

知识要点

It is useless to do sth.表示"做……是无用的"，例如：It is useless to say too many words.（说太多话是没用的。）He knew it was useless to argue with his father.（他知道跟他父亲争论是没用的。）

参考译文

一只鸟在窗户外面的笼子里。夜里，当其他鸟都睡着了，她却经常唱歌。一天晚上，蝙蝠来了。他问鸟为什么白天这么沉默，只在晚上唱歌。

鸟回答说："去年我在白天唱歌时，一个捕鸟人听到了我的歌声，用网捉到了我。从那时起，我就再也没有在白天唱过歌了。"

蝙蝠说："但是你现在已经是囚犯了，再这么做也没用了。"随后他就飞走了。

答案与解析

❶ T　由第一段第一句可知本题正确。

❷ F　由第一段第二句可知，鸟总在夜里唱歌，本题错误。

❸ T　由第二段可知本题正确。

❹ F　由第三段蝙蝠说的话可知，他认为鸟成了囚犯，就算在夜里唱歌也没用了，所以蝙蝠不认同鸟的做法，本题错误。

❺ T　结合全文，鸟住在笼子里，无法飞走，本题正确。

Passage 5 阅读短文，判断句子正（T）误（F）。

A monkey is hungry. He wants to look for something to eat. He sees many peaches on the tree. So he climbs on the peach tree and picks up the peaches. Suddenly he sees many bananas on other trees. He then jumps down and runs to the banana trees. Every banana is big and yellow. He is very happy. Then he sees many watermelons on the ground. He begins to pick up the watermelons. A hare comes up. The monkey sees the hare. Then he runs after it. In the end, the monkey gets nothing.

词汇积累		
climb /klaɪm/ v. 爬；攀登		suddenly /ˈsʌdənli/ adv. 突然地
watermelon /ˈwɔːtəmelən/ n. 西瓜		hare /heə(r)/ n. 野兔

(　　) ❶ The monkey is thirsty.

(　　) ❷ The monkey does not pick up the peaches.

(　　) ❸ Bananas are big and yellow.

(　　) ❹ The monkey loses bananas because of watermelons.

(　　) ❺ The monkey gets the hare in the end.

 知识要点

run after表示"追逐，追赶"，例如：The dog was running after a rabbit.（狗在追一只兔子。）If you run after two hares, you will catch neither.（同时追二兔，必将无所获。）

 参考译文

一只猴子饿了。他想找东西吃。他看到树上有许多桃子。于是他爬上树摘桃子。突然，他在其他树上看到许多香蕉。他随后跳下桃树，向香蕉树跑去。每根香蕉都又大又黄。他很开心。他又看到地上有许多西瓜，于是开始摘西瓜。一只野兔跑了过来。猴子看见了野兔，开始追它。最后，猴子什么也没得到。

 答案与解析

❶ F 由第一句可知，这只猴子饿了，而不是渴了，本题错误。

❷ F 由第四句可知，猴子爬上桃树摘了桃子，本题错误。

❸ T 由第七句可知本题正确。

❹ T 由倒数第五句可知本题正确。

❺ F 由最后一句可知，猴子最终什么都没得到，他并没追到野兔，本题错误。

Passage 6　阅读短文，回答问题。

One day the wind says to the sun, "Look at that man walking along the road. I can get his coat off more quickly than you can."

"We will see about that," says the sun, "I will let you try first."

So the wind tries to make the man take off his coat. He blows and blows, but the man only pulls his coat more closely around himself.

"I give up," says the wind at last. "I cannot get his coat off." Then the sun tries. He shines as hard as he can. The man soon becomes hot and takes off his coat.

词汇 积累	along /ə'lɒŋ/ *adv.* 沿着，顺着	pull /pʊl/ *v.* 拉；拽
	closely /'kləʊsli/ *adv.* 紧密地，严密地	at last 最后

❶ What do the wind and the sun want to do?

_____

❷ What does the wind do to get the man's coat off?

_____

❸ What does the man do after the wind blows?

_____

❹ What does the sun do to get the man's coat off?

_____

❺ Why does the man take off his coat?

_____

知识要点

take off表示"脱下（衣服）；摘掉（帽子等）"，例如：Now we can take off the caps.（现在我们可以摘下帽子了。）He took off his wet shoes.（他脱掉湿漉漉的鞋子。）

 参考译文

有一天，风对太阳说："看那个沿着马路走的人。我可以比你更快地让他脱下外套。"

太阳说："那我们就看看，你先来。"

接着，风尝试让那个人脱下外套。他吹啊吹啊，但那个人只把外套裹得更紧了。

"我放弃，"最后风说道。"我不能让他脱掉外套。"接着太阳开始尝试。他尽最大的力气照耀。那个人很快就觉得热了，脱下了外套。

 答案与解析

❶ They want to get the man's coat off. 本题需要对第一段的内容进行总结，大意正确即可。

❷ The wind blows and blows. 由第三段第二句可知答案。

❸ The man pulls his coat more closely around himself. 由第三段第二句可知答案。

❹ The sun shines as hard as he can. 由最后一段倒数第二句可知答案。

❺ Because he feels hot. 由最后一段最后一句可知答案。

Passage 7 阅读短文，判断句子正（T）误（F）。

A cat goes to a river every day. He wants to go fishing. But he cannot catch any fish.

One day, he goes to the river as usual. Suddenly a fish comes out. He catches the fish. He is very happy and forgets to put the fish in the basket. He dances and sings. He shouts, "I have a fish! I have a fish!" All his friends come to see him.

"Where is your fish? Let us have a look at it." his friends say.

"It's there, near the bank." the cat answers. But he cannot find the fish. When he sings and dances, the fish jumps back into the river.

词汇积累	catch /kætʃ/ v. 捕捉，捕获	usual /'juːʒuəl/ adj. 通常的，平常的
	forget /fə'get/ v. 忘记	bank /bæŋk/ n. 岸；河畔

( ) ❶ This cat wants to go swimming.

( ) ❷ This cat catches the fish.

( ) ❸ This cat puts the fish in the basket.

( ) ❹ All of the cat's friends come to see his fish.

( ) ❺ The cat eats the fish.

知识要点

as usual表示"像往常一样，照例"。例如：Steve, as usual, was the last one.（史蒂夫照例是最后一名。）He was late, as usual.（他照例迟到了。）

 参考译文

有只猫每天都去河边。他想钓鱼。但是却一条鱼都抓不到。

有一天，他像往常一样去河边。突然出现了一条鱼。他抓到了这条鱼。他很高兴，忘了把鱼放进篮子里。他又唱又跳，大喊道："我抓到了鱼！我抓到了鱼！"他的朋友都过来看。

"你的鱼在哪里？让我们看看。"他的朋友们说。

"就在河岸附近。"这只猫回答。但是他却找不到这条鱼了。在他又唱又跳的时候，这条鱼跳回了河里。

 答案与解析

❶ F 由第一段第二句可知，这只猫想钓鱼，而不是想游泳，本题错误。

❷ T 由第二段第三句可知本题正确。

❸ F 由第二段第四句可知，这只猫太开心了，忘记把鱼放进篮子里，本题错误。

❹ T 由第二段最后一句可知本题正确。

❺ F 由最后一段最后一句可知，鱼跳回了河里，所以猫并没有吃到鱼，本题错误。

Passage 阅读短文，回答问题。

One day, a monkey and a turtle ran a race. The monkey said, "I am big, I can run fast. I will win." The turtle said, "I am small. I am slow. But I will do my best." The monkey ran faster than the turtle. Then the monkey's friend, the rabbit came out. The rabbit said to the monkey, "Let's play!" The monkey thought he would win anyway. So he played with the rabbit. The turtle ran slowly. But he ran and ran. Finally the turtle won. The turtle shouted, "I won!" The monkey was still playing with the rabbit. Then the monkey found the turtle. He was very surprised. But it was too late.

词汇积累	race /reɪs/ *n.* 赛跑	win /wɪn/ *v.* 获胜
	slow /sləʊ/ *adj.* 慢的	anyway /'eniweɪ/ *adv.* 无论如何

1. Who can run faster, the monkey or the turtle?

_____

2. Why did the monkey play with the rabbit?

_____

3. Who was the winner at last?

_____

4. Did the turtle play during the race?

_____

5. How did the monkey feel when he found the turtle won?

_____

知识要点

do one's best表示"尽某人全力"，例如：I will do my best in this game.（我将在比赛中尽自己最大努力。）I do my best to take care of my grandmother.（我尽最大努力去照顾我的祖母。）

参考译文

一天，一只猴子和一只乌龟赛跑。猴子说："我很大，我能跑得很快。我会赢。"乌龟说："我很小，我慢，不过我会尽力的。"猴子跑得比乌龟快。然后猴子的朋友兔子出现了。兔子对猴子说："我们一起玩吧！"猴子认为他无论如何都会赢，于是他和兔子一起玩。乌龟慢慢地跑着。但是他跑啊跑，最后乌龟赢了。乌龟大喊道："我赢了！"猴子还在和兔子玩。然后猴子找到了乌龟。他非常惊讶，但已经太迟了。

答案与解析

① The monkey. 由第四句可知答案。

② Because the monkey thought he would win anyway. 由第七句可知答案。

③ The turtle. 由倒数第五句和第六句可知答案。

④ No, he didn't. 结合全文，乌龟虽然跑得慢，但他一直跑，本题为否定回答。

⑤ He was very surprised. 由倒数第二句可知答案。

 Passage 阅读短文，回答问题。

There is a big cat in the house. He catches many mice while they are stealing food.

One day the mice have a meeting to talk about the way to deal with the cat. Some say this, and some say that.

At last, a young mouse gets up, and says that he has a good idea.

"We could tie a bell around the neck of the cat. Then when he comes near, we can hear the sound of the bell, and run away."

Everyone approves（赞同）of this young mouse, but an old mouse gets up and says, "That is all very well, but who will tie the bell to the cat?" The mice look at each other, but nobody speaks.

词汇积累	steal /stiːl/ v. 偷，窃取	meeting /'miːtɪŋ/ n. 会议
	deal /diːl/ v. 应对	tie /taɪ/ v. 系；拴；捆

❶ What does the cat do?

＿＿＿＿＿＿＿＿

❷ What do the mice do?

＿＿＿＿＿＿＿＿

❸ What is the young mouse's good idea?

＿＿＿＿＿＿＿＿

❹ What can the mice do when they hear the sound of the bell?

＿＿＿＿＿＿＿＿

 Why does nobody speak in the end?

 知识要点

deal with表示"解决，处理，应付"，例如：Do you know how to deal with this problem?（你知道怎么应付这个难题吗？）He must deal with many difficulties.（他必须应对许多困难。）

 参考译文

从前，一所房子里面有一只大猫，他抓住了很多偷东西的老鼠。

一天，老鼠在一起开会商量如何对付这只猫。会上大家各有各的主张。

最后，一只年幼的老鼠站出来，说他有一个好主意。

"我们可以在猫的脖子上系一个铃铛，如果他来到附近，我们听到铃声就可以马上逃跑。"

大家都赞同这个建议，这时一只年长的老鼠站出来说："这的确是个绝妙的主意，但是谁来给猫的脖子上系铃铛呢？"老鼠们面面相觑，谁也没有说话。

 答案与解析

① He catches many mice while they are stealing food. 由第一段第二句可知答案。

② They have a meeting to talk about the way to deal with the cat. 由第二段第一句可知答案。

③ Tie a bell around the neck of the cat. 由第四段第一句可知答案。

④ They can run away. 由第四段第二句可知答案。

⑤ Because they do not know who will tie the bell to the cat. 由最后一段可以推测，没有人敢去系铃铛，所以没有人说话。

Passage 10 阅读短文，判断句子正（T）误（F）。

There is a naughty boy in a village. He likes telling lies. One day he wants to make fun of the farmers. So he shouts, "Wolf! Wolf! Wolf is coming!" The kind farmers are working in the field. They hear the shout, and hurry to help the boy. But when they get there, the boy says, "There isn't a wolf. I am joking." The farmers are angry and go back to their field. After a while, the boy shouts again, "Wolf! Wolf! Wolf is coming!" The farmers come and are cheated（欺骗） again. The boy laughs and laughs. Farmers say, "You tell lies. We will not believe（相信） you."

Later, a wolf really comes. The boy is very scared. "Wolf! Wolf! Wolf is coming!" the boy shouts and shouts, "Help! Help!" But no one comes. And the wolf eats the naughty boy.

| 词汇 积累 | lie /laɪ/ *n.* 谎言，谎话 | field /fiːld/ *n.* 田地 |
| | joke /dʒəʊk/ *v.* 闹着玩，说着玩 | scared /skeəd/ *adj.* 害怕的 |

( ) ❶ The boy does not like telling lies.

( ) ❷ The farmers believe the boy at first.

( ) ❸ The farmers come to the boy two times.

( ) ❹ No wolf comes.

( ) ❺ The boy runs away.

Unit 10 哲理故事

知识要点

make fun of sb.表示"取笑某人，嘲弄某人"，例如：He thinks it's clever to make fun of people.（他觉得拿别人开玩笑显得聪明。）Don't make fun of him.（别拿他开玩笑。）

参考译文

一个村庄里有一个顽皮的男孩。他喜欢说谎。有一天，他想捉弄农民们。于是他喊道："狼！狼！狼来了！"善良的农民们正在田间劳作。他们听到了呼喊声，急忙赶来帮助这个男孩。但是他们到了之后，男孩说："没有狼。我在开玩笑呢。"农民们很生气，回到了地里。过了一会儿，男孩再次大喊："狼！狼！狼来了！"农民们来了，又被骗了。男孩大笑不止。农民们说："你在撒谎。我们不会再相信你了。"

之后，狼真的来了。这个男孩很害怕。"狼！狼！狼来了！"男孩喊道，"救命！救命！"但是谁也没来。狼吃了那个调皮的男孩。

答案与解析

❶ F 由第一段第二句可知，男孩喜欢说谎，本题错误。

❷ T 由第一段可知，前两次男孩撒谎的时候，农民们都来了，他们刚开始是相信男孩的，本题正确。

❸ T 由第一段可知，农民们在听到男孩的呼喊后，去了两次，本题正确。

❹ F 由第二段第一句可知，狼真的来了，本题错误。

❺ F 故事最后，狼来了，因为已经没有人相信男孩了，男孩被狼吃掉了，本题错误。

175

Passage **11** 阅读短文，选择最佳答案。

Mr. White looks out of his window. There is a boy at the other side of the street. The boy takes some bread out of a bag and begins eating it. There is a very thin dog in the street, too. The boy says to it, "I'll give you some bread." The dog is hungry and goes to the boy, but he does not give it any bread. He kicks the dog. It runs away, and the boy laughs.

Then Mr. White comes out of his house and says to the boy, "I'll give you money." The boy is happy and says, "Yes." "Come here." Mr. White says. The boy goes to him, but Mr. White does not give him money. He hits him with a stick. The boy cries and says, "Why do you hit me? I do not ask you for any money." "No," Mr. White says, "And the dog does not ask you for any bread, but you kick it."

词汇 积累	street /striːt/ *n.* 街道	thin /θɪn/ *adj.* 瘦的
	kick /kɪk/ *v.* 踢	stick /stɪk/ *n.* 木棍

( ) **1** In the first paragraph, where is Mr. White?

    A. He is in his house.   B. He is at school.

    C. He is in the shop.   D. He is on the street.

( ) **2** What does the boy do?

    A. The boy gives the dog some bread.

    B. The boy kicks the dog.

C. The boy touches the dog.

D. The bog takes the dog home.

(　　) ❸ Why does Mr. White hit the boy?

A. Because he is bad.

B. Because he gives the boy money.

C. Because he wants to teach the boy a lesson.

D. Because he has nothing to do.

(　　) ❹ How does Mr. White think of the boy?

A. He thinks the boy is good.

B. He thinks the boy is nice.

C. He thinks the boy is great.

D. He thinks the boy should give bread to the dog.

(　　) ❺ What do you know from this story?

A. We should do what we say.

B. We should not give bread to dogs.

C. We should hit others.

D. We should not want others' money.

 知识要点

　　some和any都表示"一些"，some通常用于肯定句，例如：Have some more vegetables.（再吃点蔬菜吧。）any通常用于疑问句和否定句，例如：Are there any stamps?（有邮票吗？）I didn't eat any meat.（我一点肉也没吃。）

 参考译文

　　怀特先生正向窗外看。有一个男孩正站在街对面。这个男孩从包里拿出了一个面包开始吃。街上还有一只很瘦的狗。男孩对狗说："我给你些

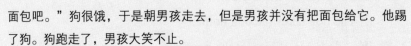

面包吧。"狗很饿，于是朝男孩走去，但是男孩并没有把面包给它。他踢了狗。狗跑走了，男孩大笑不止。

随后怀特先生走出家，对男孩说："我给你些钱吧。"男孩很开心，说："好的。""过来。"怀特先生说。男孩朝他走去，但是怀特先生并没有给男孩钱。他用木棍打了男孩。男孩哭喊着："你为什么要打我？我并没有向你要钱啊。""你没有，"怀特先生说，"但是那只狗也没有向你要面包，但你还是踢了它。"

 答案与解析

❶ A　由第二段第一句话可知，怀特先生在看到男孩的行为之后，从自己的家走了出来，即怀特先生之前在家里，A正确。

❷ B　由第一段倒数第二句和第三句可知，男孩骗狗过来后，并没有给它面包，而是踢了它，B正确。

❸ C　由第二段可知，怀特先生在看到男孩不讲信用的行为之后，决定以相同的方式对待男孩，让他明白自己行为的不妥，给他一次教训，C符合大意。A和D在文中并未提及。怀特先生并不是因为给了男孩钱才打他，B错误。

❹ D　由对第三题的分析可知本题选D。A、B、C均不符合文意。

❺ A　这个故事告诉我们要守信用，不能欺负弱小，A正确。本文并非讨论不应该给狗面包，B错误。文章想要表达的是不能随意欺负弱小，C错误。文章没有涉及是否应该要别人的钱财，D错误。

Part 2

★

真题实战

Unit 01 组合训练 1

Hello! My name is Mike. I'm a boy. I'm a pupil. I'm from Canada. I'm eleven years old. I have three new friends. They are Jerry, Daisy and Sun Wei. Jerry is a boy. He is thirteen years old. He has two cute dogs. Daisy is a girl. She is twelve years old. She is from the UK. Sun Wei is my teacher. She is from China. She is a beautiful teacher. She likes reading books. She has twenty books in her desk.

（安徽省合肥市）

( ) ❶ How old is Mike?

    A. He is 11.   B. He is 12.

    C. He is 13.   D. He is 14.

( ) ❷ Is Jerry thirteen years old?

    A. Yes, he is.   B. Yes, she is.

    C. No, he isn't.   D. No, she isn't.

( ) ❸ Where is Daisy from?

    A. She's from Canada.   B. She's from the UK.

    C. He's from China.   D. He's from the UK.

( ) ❹ Is Sun Wei a student?

    A. Yes, he is.   B. Yes, she is.

    C. No, he isn't.   D. No, she isn't.

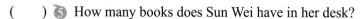

( ) How many books does Sun Wei have in her desk?

A. She has 10 books.   B. She has 15 books.

C. She has 20 books.   D. She has 25 books.

 参考译文

　　你好！我的名字叫迈克。我是个男孩。我是个小学生。我来自加拿大。我11岁了。我有三个新朋友。他们是杰里、黛西和孙薇。杰里是个男孩。他13岁。他有两只可爱的狗。黛西是个女孩，她12岁，来自英国。孙薇是我的老师。她来自中国。她是一位漂亮的老师。她喜欢读书，她的桌子里有20本书。

答案与解析

❶ A　定位到介绍迈克的句子，可知迈克11岁，A正确。

❷ A　定位到介绍杰里的句子，可知杰瑞13岁，本题为肯定回答，A正确。

❸ B　定位到介绍黛西的句子，可知黛西来自英国，B正确。

❹ D　定位到介绍孙薇的句子，可知孙薇是老师，本题为否定回答，D正确。

❺ C　由最后一句可知选C。

 Passage ② 阅读短文，选择最佳答案。

What's in My Pencil Box?

I have a pencil box. It's blue. There are lots of things in it. There are two red pens and a black pen. I like the black pen. I have five pencils. They are brown. I like the white ruler best.

（天津市）

(　　) ❶ The pencil box is _____.

　　A. yellow　　　　　B. blue　　　　　　C. black

(　　) ❷ I have _____ pen(s).

　　A. 3　　　　　　　B. 2　　　　　　　　C. 1

(　　) ❸ There are _____ pencils.

　　A. two red　　　　B. five brown　　　　C. five black

(　　) ❹ The ruler is _____.

　　A. red　　　　　　B. black　　　　　　　C. white

(　　) ❺ How many kinds of colours are mentioned in this passage?

　　A. Three.　　　　　B. Four.　　　　　　C. Five.

参考译文

我的文具盒里有什么?

　　我有一个铅笔盒。它是蓝色的。它里面放了很多东西。里面有两支红钢笔和一支黑钢笔。我喜欢黑钢笔。我有五支铅笔,它们是棕色的。我最喜欢白色的尺子。

答案与解析

❶ B　由第二句可知选B。

❷ A　由第四句可知,文具盒里一共有三支钢笔,A正确。

❸ B　由倒数第二句和倒数第三句可知选B。

❹ C　由最后一句可知选C。

❺ C　综合全文,提到了 "blue, red, black, brown, white" 共五种颜色,C正确。

Passage **3** 阅读短文，判断句子正（T）误（F）。

Hello, I'm Mike. I have a nice room. I have a desk, a chair and a bed in my room. My cap and my bag are on the desk. The cap is blue. A pencil box is in my bag. A ball is under the chair. It's black and white. I have a toy box. It's near the bed. I like my room very much.

（广东省深圳市）

( ) ❶ Mike's room is nice.

( ) ❷ Mike's cap and bag are on the desk.

( ) ❸ Mike's ball is on the chair.

( ) ❹ Mike doesn't like his room.

 参考译文

你好，我是迈克。我有一个漂亮的房间。我的房间里有一张桌子，一把椅子和一张床。我的帽子和包在桌子上。帽子是蓝色的。我的包里有一个文具盒。椅子下面有一个球，它是黑白相间的。我有一个玩具箱，它在床旁边。我非常喜欢我的房间。

🔍 答案与解析

❶ T 由第二句可知本题正确。

❷ T 由第四句可知本题正确。

❸ F 由倒数第五句可知，球在椅子下面，而不是在椅子上面，本题错误。

❹ F 由最后一句可知，迈克非常喜欢自己的房间，本题错误。

 Passage ❹ 阅读短文，判断句子正（T）误（F）。

Teddy and Kitty are good friends. They often go to school together. In the morning, Teddy gets up at six and has breakfast at seven. He likes to eat noodles and eggs. Kitty gets up late. She often drinks milk for breakfast. Kitty likes pandas and cats, but Teddy likes monkeys. They both like bears. They like to read books in the evening.

（北京市）

(   ) ❶ Teddy gets up at six in the morning.

(   ) ❷ Kitty likes to eat noodles and eggs.

(   ) ❸ Kitty likes pandas, cats and bears.

(   ) ❹ Teddy likes dogs.

(   ) ❺ Kitty and Teddy like to read books in the evening.

 参考译文

　　特迪和基蒂是好朋友。他们经常一起去上学。早晨，特迪六点起床，七点吃早饭。他喜欢吃面条和鸡蛋。基蒂起床晚，她早餐经常喝牛奶。基蒂喜欢熊猫和猫，但是特迪喜欢猴子。他们两人都喜欢熊。他们喜欢在晚上读书。

答案与解析

❶ T 由第三句可知本题正确。

❷ F 由第四句可知，是特迪喜欢吃面条和鸡蛋，而不是基蒂，本题错误。

❸ T 由倒数第二句和第三句可知，基蒂喜欢熊猫和猫，两人都喜欢熊，本题正确。

❹ F 由倒数第三句可知，特迪喜欢猴子，而不是狗，本题错误。

❺ T 由最后一句可知本题正确。

 Passage ❺ 阅读短文，选择合适的词完成句子。

Hello! I'm Taotao. I'm fourteen years old. I like apples. This is Dongdong. He's thirteen years old. He likes watermelons. This is Yuanyuan. She's eleven years old. She's thin. She likes pears. This is Feifei. She's twelve years old. She likes bananas. This is Mingming. He's fifteen years old. He's cute. He likes grapes.

（浙江省杭州市）

twelve	eleven	fourteen	fifteen	thirteen
grapes	pears	watermelons	apples	bananas

❶ Taotao is _____ . He likes _____ .

❷ Dongdong is _____ . He likes _____ .

❸ Yuanyuan is _____ . She likes _____ .

❹ Feifei is _____ . She likes _____ .

❺ Mingming is _____ . He likes _____ .

 参考译文

　　你好！我是涛涛。我14岁。我喜欢苹果。这是东东。他13岁。他喜欢西瓜。这是圆圆。她11岁。她很瘦。她喜欢梨。这是菲菲。她12岁。她喜欢香蕉。这是明明。他15岁。他很可爱。他喜欢葡萄。

答案与解析

❶ fourteen; apples　由文中对涛涛的介绍可知答案。

❷ thirteen; watermelons　由文中对东东的介绍可知答案。

❸ eleven; pears　由文中对圆圆的介绍可知答案。

❹ twelve; bananas　由文中对菲菲的介绍可知答案。

❺ fifteen; grapes　由文中对明明的介绍可知答案。

Unit 02 组合训练 2

Hello! My name is Jack. I'm from the UK. I'm eleven years old. I'm a student. I'm short and thin. I have big eyes and big ears. I have a brother, Jimmy. He's fourteen years old. He's tall and thin. He has small eyes and big ears. We like fruit. I like strawberries. I don't like oranges. Jimmy likes strawberries, watermelons and oranges. I wash some grapes. I put them on the plate. We eat together.

（河南省郑州市）

( ) **1** Jack is _____ years old.

    A. 11   B. 13   C. 14

( ) **2** Jack and Jimmy are from _____.

    A. the UK   B. the USA   C. Canada

( ) **3** Jimmy is _____.

    A. short and thin   B. short and fat   C. tall and thin

( ) **4** Jack and Jimmy have _____.

    A. big eyes   B. big ears   C. small ears

( ) **5** Jack and Jimmy like _____.

    A. strawberries

    B. strawberries and oranges

    C. watermelons

Part 2 真题实战

 参考译文

你好！我是杰克。我来自英国。我11岁。我是一名学生。我又矮又瘦。我的眼睛大，耳朵大。我有一个哥哥，名字是吉米。他14岁。他又高又瘦。他的眼睛小，耳朵大。我们喜欢水果。我喜欢草莓。我不喜欢橙子。吉米喜欢草莓、西瓜和橙子。我洗了一些葡萄，把它们放在盘子里。我们一起吃。

答案与解析

1 A 由第四句可知选A。

2 A 由第三句可知，杰克来自英国。由第八句可知，杰克和吉米是兄弟。因此，他们两人都来自英国，A正确。

3 C 定位到文章对吉米的介绍，C正确。

4 B 定位到文章对杰克和吉米的介绍，杰克和吉米都有一对大耳朵，B正确。

5 A 定位到文章对杰克和吉米喜欢的水果的介绍，杰克喜欢草莓，不喜欢橙子；吉米喜欢草莓、西瓜和橙子。因此，他们两个都喜欢的是草莓，A正确。

Passage 2 阅读短文，选择最佳答案。

Hello. My name's Coco. Nice to meet you. I'm five years old. Look at me. I have one eye, three ears, four arms and two legs. Haha! I am a monster.

Today is my birthday. I'd like some juice and cake. Look! I have many gifts. There is a black bag, a blue pencil box, a monkey eraser and so on. What's this? Oh, it's a yellow yo-yo. I like it.

（浙江省温州市）

( ) ❶ What am I?

　　A. I am a rooster. 　　B. I am a monster. 　　C. I am a bird.

( ) ❷ I am _____ years old

　　A. 3 　　B. 4 　　C. 5

( ) ❸ I'd like some _____.

　　A. juice and bread 　　B. juice and cake 　　C. milk and cake

( ) ❹ I like the _____ yo-yo.

　　A. black 　　B. blue 　　C. yellow

( ) ❺ I have a monkey _____.

　　A. eraser 　　B. pencil box 　　C. bag

✏️ **参考译文**

　　你好。我叫可可。很高兴认识你。我今年五岁。看看我。我有一只眼睛，三只耳朵，四只胳膊和两条腿。哈哈！我是一只怪兽。

Part 2 真题实战

今天是我的生日。我想要一些果汁和蛋糕。看！我有很多礼物。有一个黑色的包，一个蓝色的铅笔盒，一个猴子橡皮等等。这是什么？ 哦，是黄色的溜溜球。我喜欢它。

 答案与解析

1 B 由第一段最后一句可知选B。

2 C 由第一段第四句可知选C。

3 B 由第二段第二句可知选B。

4 C 由第二段最后两句可知选C。

5 A 由第二段第五句可知选A。

 Passage 3 阅读短文，判断句子正（T）误（F）。

My name is Jim Green. I am twelve. I play football on Sundays. Football is my favourite sport. I have art on Mondays. I like drawing pictures. This is my picture. This monkey is fat and tall. The summer is coming. Daming and I go swimming in summer. I am in Yantai. It's cold in winter.

（天津市）

( ) 1 Jim Green is 11.

( ) 2 Jim Green's favourite sport is football.

(   ) ③ The monkey in Jim Green's picture is thin and short.

(   ) ④ Daming and Jim Green go swimming in autumn.

(   ) ⑤ Yantai is cold in winter.

 参考译文

    我叫吉姆·格林。我12岁。我在星期天踢足球。足球是我最喜欢的运动。星期一我会上绘画课。我喜欢画画。这是我的画。上面的这只猴子又胖又高。夏天快到了。大明和我夏天会去游泳。我住在烟台。这里冬天很冷。

 答案与解析

① F   由第二句可知，吉姆·格林12岁，不是11岁，本题错误。

② T   由第四句可知本题正确。

③ F   由倒数第五句可知，吉姆·格林画的猴子又胖又高，不是又瘦又矮，本题错误。

④ F   由倒数第三句可知，大明和吉姆·格林在夏天去游泳，而不是秋天，本题错误。

⑤ T   由最后两句可知本题正确。

Passage 4　阅读对话，判断句子正（T）误（F）。

Nancy: Good morning, Su Hai.

Su Hai: Good morning, Nancy.

Nancy: What's that behind the chair?

Su Hai: It's a green bag.

Nancy: Is it your bag?

Su Hai: No, it isn't. My bag is red. I think it's Su Yang's.

Nancy: Where's Su Yang?

Su Hai: She's in the computer room.

（江苏省苏州市）

(　　) ❶ It's in the morning.

(　　) ❷ The green bag is Su Hai's.

(　　) ❸ Su Hai's bag is red.

(　　) ❹ Su Hai's bag is behind the chair.

(　　) ❺ Su Yang is in the library.

 参考译文

南希：早上好，苏海。

苏海：早上好，南希。

南希：椅子后面是什么？

苏海：是一个绿色的包。

南希：是你的包吗？

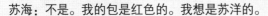

苏海：不是。我的包是红色的。我想是苏洋的。

南希：苏洋在哪里？

苏海：她在计算机室里。

 答案与解析

❶ T　由两人打招呼时用的 "Good morning." 可知，这段对话发生在早上，本题正确。

❷ F　由对话中苏海所说的 "I think it's Su Yang's." 可知，这个绿色的包应该是苏洋的，本题错误。

❸ T　由对话中苏海所说的 "My bag is red." 可知，苏海的包是红色的，本题正确。

❹ F　苏海的包是红色的，椅子后面的包是绿色的，本题错误。

❺ F　由对话中苏海所说的 "She's in the computer room." 可知，苏洋在计算机室，而不是在图书馆，本题错误。

 Passage 5 阅读短文，回答问题。

Tom is a good boy. He is tall. His favourite colour is blue. He likes sports. In spring, he rides a bike in the park. In summer, he plays basketball with his friends under the tree. In autumn, he goes fishing with his dad by the lake. In winter, he plays in the snow with his friends at school. He is happy every day.

（山东省烟台市）

❶ What's Tom's favourite colour?

_____

❷ What does Tom like?

_____

❸ What does Tom do in spring?

_____

❹ Whom does Tom go fishing with?

_____

❺ Where does Tom play in the snow in winter?

_____

 参考译文

　　汤姆是一个好孩子。他很高。他最喜欢的颜色是蓝色。他喜欢运动。在春天，他在公园里骑自行车。在夏天，他和他的朋友们在树下打篮球。在秋天，他和他的爸爸在湖边钓鱼。在冬天，他和他的朋友们在学校的雪地里玩耍。他每天都很快乐。

 答案与解析

❶ Tom's favourite colour is blue./It's blue.　由第三句可知答案。

❷ He likes sports.　由第四句可知答案。

❸ He rides a bike in the park.　由第五句可知答案。

❹ His dad.　由倒数第三句可知答案。

❺ At school.　由倒数第二句可知答案。

Unit 03　组合训练 3

Passage 1 阅读短文，选择最佳答案。

I have two beautiful pictures in my photo album. Look at the first picture. It is a picture of my family. My parents and I are smiling in the picture. My parents love me and I love them, too. We have a happy family.

There are only two people in the second picture. They are my father and my mother. Where am I? I was not born at that time.

（北京市）

(　　) ❶ -How many beautiful pictures do I have?

-I have _____.

A. one　　　　　　　B. two　　　　　　　C. three

(　　) ❷ -What is the first picture?

-The first picture is about my _____.

A. family　　　　　　B. class　　　　　　C. friends

(　　) ❸ We have a _____ family.

A. happy　　　　　　B. good　　　　　　C. bad

(　　) ❹ -How many people are there in the second picture?

-There are _____ people.

A. one　　　　　　　B. two　　　　　　　C. three

(　　) ❺ My father and my _____ are in the second picture.

A. brother　　　　　B. aunt　　　　　　C. mother

参考译文

　　我的相册里有两张漂亮的照片。看第一张，是我的全家福。照片里我和爸爸妈妈都在微笑。爸爸妈妈很爱我，我也很爱他们。我们有一个快乐的家庭。

　　第二张照片里只有两个人。他们是我的爸爸和妈妈。我在哪儿呢？我那时候还没有出生。

答案与解析

❶ B　由第一段第一句可知选B。

❷ A　由第一段第三句可知选A。

❸ A　由第一段最后一句可知选A。

❹ B　由第二段第一句可知选B。

❺ C　由第二段第二句可知选C。

　Passage ❷　阅读短文，选择最佳答案。

Betty and Kitty are twin sisters. They are 10 years old. Betty likes oranges, and Kitty likes apples. They're in the library now.

Betty: Would you like an orange?

Kitty: No, thank you. Don't eat here.

（江苏省南京市）

(　　) ❶ Betty and Kitty are _____.

        A. boys   B. girls

(　　) ❷ How old is Betty?

        A. Five.   B. Ten.

(　　) ❸ Betty likes _____.

        A. oranges   B. apples

(　　) ❹ Where are they?

        A. On the farm.   B. In the library.

(　　) ❺ Don't _____ in the library.

        A. eat   B. read

✏️ 参考译文

　　贝蒂和基蒂是双胞胎姐妹。她们10岁了。贝蒂喜欢橙子，基蒂喜欢苹果。她们现在在图书馆。

　　贝蒂：你要橙子吗?

　　基蒂：不，谢谢。不要在这里吃东西。

🔍 答案与解析

❶ B　由第一段第一句可知，贝蒂和基蒂是双胞胎姐妹，B正确。

❷ B　由第一段第二句可知选B。

❸ A　由第一段第三句可知选A。

❹ B　由第一段最后一句可知选B。

❺ A　由基蒂对贝蒂说的"Don't eat here."可知，不要在图书馆吃东西，A正确。

Part 2 真题实战

Passage 3 阅读短文，判断句子正（T）误（F）。

Look! This is my room. The toy car is under the desk. The toy boat is on the desk. My cat is under the chair. It's black. It has two big eyes. I like it very much. Where is my new pencil box? Is it on the desk? No, it isn't. It's on the chair. The books are on the chair, too.

（江西省南昌市）

(   ) ❶ The toy car is in the desk.

(   ) ❷ The toy boat is on the desk.

(   ) ❸ My cat is yellow.

(   ) ❹ My pencil box is on the desk.

(   ) ❺ My books are on the chair.

 参考译文

看！这是我的房间。玩具车在桌子下面。玩具船在桌子上面。我的猫在椅子下面。猫是黑色的。它有两只大眼睛。我非常喜欢它。我的新文具盒在哪里？在桌子上吗？不。它在椅子上。书也在椅子上。

 答案与解析

❶ F   由第三句可知，玩具汽车在桌子下面，而不是在桌子里面，本题错误。

② T 由第四句可知本题正确。

③ F 由第五句和第六句可知，"我"的猫是黑色的，而不是黄色的，本题错误。

④ F 定位到文中对文具盒的描述可知，文具盒在椅子上，而不是在桌子上，本题错误。

⑤ T 由最后一句可知本题正确。

 Passage 阅读短文，判断句子正（T）误（F）。

Come on, children! Let's go to the zoo. Look! This is a panda. It's black and white. It's so fat. Look at the cute monkey! It has a long tail. What's that? The body is so big. The head is so small. The tail is so short. Oh, it's a big bird.

（山东省济南市）

( )   **①** Let's go to the school, children!
( )   **②** The panda is black and white.
( )   **③** The monkey has a long tail.
( )   **④** The bird has a big body.
( )   **⑤** The bird is small.

 参考译文

快来，孩子们！我们去动物园。看！这是一只熊猫，它是黑白相间的。它真胖。看看那只可爱的猴子！它有一条长长的尾巴。那是什么？身子大大的，头小小的，尾巴短短的。哦，是一只大鸟。

Part 2 真题实战

 答案与解析

❶ F 由第二句可知，"我们"要去动物园，而不是去学校，本题错误。

❷ T 由第五句可知本题正确。

❸ T 由第八句可知本题正确。

❹ T 由倒数第四句可知本题正确。

❺ F 由最后一句可知，鸟很大，本题错误。

**Passage ** 阅读短文，回答问题。

Of all the teachers, I love my English teacher best.

He is thirty years old. We all call him Mr. Li. He is not tall, but a little fat. He wears a pair of glasses. He is very kind and patient（耐心的）. We all like him and his lessons. In his class, we feel very happy. He always makes his English lessons interesting. We feel English is very easy, and also very interesting.

This is my English teacher.

（北京市）

❶ Do I love my English teacher?

_____

❷ How old is my English teacher?

_____

3 What does my English teacher wear?

_____

4 How is Mr. Li?

_____

5 Do the students like their English lessons?

_____

 参考译文

　　在所有的老师中，我最喜欢我的英语老师。

　　他30岁了。我们都叫他李老师。他不高，但有点胖。他戴着一副眼镜。他很友善，也很有耐心。我们都喜欢他和他的课。在他的课上，我们感到很高兴。他总是使他的英语课很有趣。我们觉得英语很简单，也很有趣。

　　这就是我的英语老师。

 答案与解析

1 Yes, I do. 　结合全文可知本题为肯定回答。

2 He is thirty years old. 　由第二段第一句可知答案。

3 He wears a pair of glasses. 　由第二段第四句可知答案。

4 He is very kind and patient. 　由第二段第五句可知答案。

5 Yes, they do. 　由第二段最后四句可知答案。

Unit 04　组合训练 4

 Passage 1 阅读对话，选择最佳答案。

P1: Welcome to my home, Yang Ling.

P2: Thank you, Helen. Your house is big and nice. What's that on the table? Is it a dog?

P1: No. It's a toy pig.

P2: How nice! Are these oranges on the table?

P1: No. They are sweets. Have a taste.

P2: Yummy! Thank you. What are these on the sofa?

P1: They're toy cars.

P2: How lovely!

（山东省济南市）

(　　) ❶ _____ invites（邀请）_____ to her house.

　　A. Yang Ling; Helen　　B. Helen; Yang Ling　　C. Yang Ling; Linda

(　　) ❷ Is Yang Ling's house big?

　　A. No, it isn't.　　B. Yes, it is.　　C. I don't know.

(　　) ❸ Where is the toy pig?

　　A. On the sofa.　　B. Under the table.　　C. On the table.

(　　) ❹ What are these on the table?

　　A. They are oranges.　　B. They are sweets.　　C. They are toy cars.

(　　) ❺ Are the toy cars on the sofa?

　　A. Yes, they are.　　B. No, these aren't.　　C. No, they aren't.

参考译文

P1：欢迎来到我家，杨玲。

P2：谢谢你，海伦。你的房子又大又漂亮。桌子上是什么？是狗吗？

P1：不是。这是玩具猪。

P2：真好看！桌子上的那些东西是橙子吗？

P1：不，是糖果。尝一尝。

P2：好吃！谢谢你。沙发上这些是什么？

P1：是玩具车。

P2：真可爱！

答案与解析

① B　由对话的前两句可知，杨玲到海伦家去做客，B正确。

② C　对话中谈论的是海伦的房子又大又好，并没有提到杨玲的房子，C正确。

③ C　定位到对话中谈论玩具猪的句子，可知选C。

④ B　定位到对话中谈论桌子上有什么物品的句子，可知选B。

⑤ A　定位到对话中谈论沙发上有什么物品的句子，可知选A。

Passage 2 阅读对话，选择最佳答案。

Tiger: Good afternoon, Mrs. Rabbit. Let me eat you.

Rabbit: Don't eat me, Mr. Tiger. I'm old. That mouse is younger than me.

Tiger: Miss Mouse, Miss Mouse, let me eat you.

Mouse: Oh, no. Many birds are standing over there.

Tiger: Birds, I will eat you. You are my dinner.

Birds: You are bad. We can fly, can you?

Tiger: No, I can't. But where is my dinner? Who can tell me?

（湖北省黄冈市）

( )❶ The tiger is _____.

　　A. full　　　　　B. hungry　　　　C. happy

( )❷ The tiger doesn't eat the rabbit, because there is a _____ over there.

　　A. deer　　　　B. bird　　　　　C. mouse

( )❸ The tiger doesn't eat the mouse, because there are many _____ over there.

　　A. goats　　　　B. ducks　　　　C. birds

( )❹ Can the birds fly?

　　A. No, they can.　　B. Yes, they can.　　C. No, they can't.

( )❺ The tiger can't fly. He _____ at last.

　　A. eats dinner

　　B. eats the rabbit

　　C. doesn't have dinner

参考译文

老虎：下午好，兔子夫人。我要吃了你。

兔子：别吃我，老虎先生。我很老了，那只老鼠比我年轻。

老虎：老鼠小姐，老鼠小姐，我要吃了你。

老鼠：哦，别。有很多鸟儿站在那边。

老虎：鸟儿们，我要吃了你们。你们是我的晚餐。

小鸟：你太坏了。我们会飞，你会吗？

老虎：不，我不会。但是我的晚餐在哪儿呢？谁能告诉我？

答案与解析

① B 结合全文，老虎在寻找晚餐，可以推测他肚子很饿，B正确。

② C 由兔子夫人说的话可知，她建议老虎去吃老鼠，C正确。

③ C 由老鼠小姐说的话可知，她建议老虎去吃站在那边的鸟儿，C正确。

④ B 由鸟儿说的话可知，他们会飞，B正确。注意A有语法错误。

⑤ C 由最后一句老虎说的话可知，他没有吃到晚餐，C正确。

Passage 3 阅读对话，判断句子正（T）误（F）。

Mr. Li: Good afternoon, class.

Class: Good afternoon, Mr. Li.

Mr. Li: Sit down, please.

Liu Tao: Sorry, Mr. Li. I'm late.

Mr. Li: Come in, please. Don't look at the window, Mike.

Open your book, please.

Mike: OK. But I can't find my book.

Mr. Li: Is it in your schoolbag?

Mike: No, it isn't.

Mr. Li: Look! Your book is behind the chair.

Mike: Yes, thank you.

（江苏省南通市）

(　　) ❶ It's in class.

(　　) ❷ Mike is late for school.

(　　) ❸ Mike looks at the window.

(　　) ❹ Liu Tao can't find his book.

(　　) ❺ The book is behind the chair.

✏ 参考译文

李老师：下午好，上课。

同学们：下午好，李老师。

李老师：请坐。

刘涛：对不起，李老师。我迟到了。

李老师：请进。迈克，别看窗户那边了。请打开你的书。

迈克：好的。但是我找不到我的书了。

李老师：在你的书包里吗？

迈克：没有。

李老师：看！你的书在椅子后面。

迈克：是的，谢谢。

答案与解析

❶ T 由对话开头李老师和同学们打招呼的内容可知，这段对话发生在课堂上，本题正确。

❷ F 对话中是刘涛说自己迟到了，而不是迈克，本题错误。

❸ T 对话中李老师提醒迈克不要往窗户那边看，本题正确。

❹ F 对话中是迈克说找不到书，而不是刘涛找不到书，本题错误。

❺ T 由对话结尾李老师和迈克的话可知本题正确。

 Passage 阅读短文，判断句子正（T）误（F）。

Danny and Jenny are hungry. Danny wants to have donuts（甜甜圈）, hamburgers and juice. Jenny wants to eat dumplings and chicken. In a restaurant, Danny buys one donut, two hamburgers and one glass of juice. The food costs Danny twenty *yuan*. Jenny eats dumplings and chicken. The food costs Jenny nineteen *yuan*. Now, they are happy.

（河南省郑州市）

( ) ❶ Danny is hungry.

( ) ❷ Danny wants to have donuts, hamburgers and milk.

( ) ❸ Jenny eats chicken at home.

( ) ❹ The food costs Jenny twenty *yuan*.

( ) ❺ They are happy now.

参考译文

　　丹尼和珍妮都很饿。丹尼想吃甜甜圈和汉堡，喝果汁。珍妮想吃饺子和鸡肉。在餐馆里，丹尼买了一个甜甜圈，两个汉堡和一杯果汁。这些食物花了丹尼20元。珍妮吃了饺子和鸡肉。这些食物花了珍妮19元。现在他们很开心。

答案与解析

　❶ T　由第一句可知，丹尼和珍妮两人肚子都很饿，本题正确。

　❷ F　由第二句可知，丹尼想喝果汁而不是牛奶，本题错误。

　❸ F　由第四句中的"in a restaurant"可知，他们是在餐馆吃的食物，而不是在家中，本题错误。

　❹ F　由倒数第二句可知，珍妮吃饭花了19元，本题错误。

　❺ T　由最后一句可知本题正确。

Passage ❺ 阅读短文，回答问题。

　　Today is Alice's birthday. It's very cold outside. But it is warm in Alice's home. She is having a birthday party with her good friends. There is a big round birthday cake on the table. Her friends give their birthday gifts to Alice. Mary gives Alice a nice robot. The robot can sing and dance. Ann gives her a toy panda. It's soft and lovely. Kitty gives her a hat. It's warm and nice. Alice likes all the gifts. She is happy!

（上海市）

① What day is it today?

_____

② Is it warm outside?

_____

③ How is Alice's home?

_____

④ What is on the table?

_____

⑤ Does Alice like all the gifts?

_____

 参考译文

　　今天是艾丽斯的生日。外面很冷。但是艾丽斯的家里很暖和。她正在和她的好朋友们举行一个生日聚会。桌子上有一个又大又圆的生日蛋糕。她的朋友们给艾丽斯送了她们的生日礼物。玛丽给了艾丽斯一个漂亮的机器人。这个机器人会唱歌和跳舞。安给了她一个玩具熊猫。它柔软又可爱。基蒂给了她一顶帽子。它暖和又漂亮。艾丽斯喜欢所有的礼物。她很快乐！

 答案与解析

① Today is Alice's birthday.　由第一句可知答案。

② No, it isn't.　由第二句可知，外面很冷，本题为否定回答。

③ It is warm.　由第三句可知答案。

④ There is a big round birthday cake on the table.　由第五句可知答案。

⑤ Yes, she does.　由倒数第二句可知，艾丽斯喜欢所有的礼物，本题为肯定回答。

NOTE